Baptising Babies
&
Clearing Gutters

Baptising Babies

&

Clearing Gutters

A Fresh Appraisal of the Permanent Diaconate

by

Bridie Stringer

First Published by Matthew James Publishing
www.matthewjamespublishing.com

ISBN: 978-0-9574962-4-8

© 2013 Bridie Stringer
The moral rights of the author have been asserted

Apart from any fair dealing for the purpose of research, or private study, or criticism or review as permitted under the Copyright, Designs and Patents Act, 1988, this publication may only be reproduced, stored or transmitted in any form, or by any means, with the prior permission of the publisher, or in the case of reprographic reproduction, in accordance with the terms of licences issued by the Copyright Licensing Agency. Inquiries concerning reproduction outside those terms should be sent to the publisher.

Every effort was made to ensure that website references were accurate and accessible at the time of publication. Matthew James Publishing Ltd cannot take any responsibility or liability for a referenced website being unavailable due to technical or other reasons.

Matthew James Publishing Ltd is not responsible for and has no control over external website references and takes no responsibility for any loss or damage suffered as a result of using the referenced websites, or as a result of using the information published on any of the pages of the referenced websites.

Design and typesetting by WORDS BY DESIGN
Printed in England by Berforts Information Press Ltd

Cover image of leaves reproduced by permission of Cambridge Guttering Services.
Cover image of baptism copyright © Elisabetta Figus - Fotolia.com
Back cover image of the washing of the feet of seafarers on Maundy Thursday reproduced by permission of Apostolate of the Sea chaplain, Deacon Roger Stone.

Preface and Acknowledgements

I would like to gratefully acknowledge the following who have granted permission for their published works to be explored and cited:

Extracts from various pages and posts on www.vatican.va © Libreria Editrice Vaticana, 2013 – used with permission from Libreria Editrice Vaticana.

Extracts from the documents of Vatican II are from *Vatican Council II: Constitutions, Decrees, Declarations: The Basic Sixteen Documents*, edited by Austin Flannery, O.P.; permission granted by Publisher - Dominican Publications, www.dominicanpublications.com.

Extracts from *Women and Early Christianity* (1987) © Susanne Heine, permission granted by Publisher - SCM.

Extracts from *The Ordination of Women in the Catholic Church – Unmasking a Cuckoo's Egg Tradition* (2001) © John Wijngaards used by permission of Darton Longman and Todd.

Extracts from www.earlychristianwitings.com used by permission of Peter Kirby.

Extracts from *The Diaconate – A Full and Equal Order* (1994) © James Monroe Barnett, permission granted by Publisher - Trinity Press International, an imprint of Bloomsbury Publishing Plc.

Extracts from *Focus on Leadership: Servant-Leadership for the Twenty-First Century*, Larry C. Spears (Editor), Michele Lawrence (Editor), © 2001, permission granted by Publisher - John Wiley and Sons.

Extracts from *Theology of the Diaconate - The State of the Question* (2005) © Richard R. Gaillardetz, permission granted by Publisher - Paulist Press International, U.S.

Extracts from *Deacons and the Church* (2002) © John Collins, permission granted by Publisher – Gracewing Ltd.

Extracts from *The Early Christian Fathers – A Selection from the Writings of the Fathers from St Clement of Rome to Athanasius* (1969) Edited by Henry Bettenson, permission granted by Publisher - Oxford University Press

Extracts from *Priest and Bishop – Biblical Reflections* (1999) © Raymond E. Brown, permission granted by Publisher - Wipf and Stock Publishers. www.wipfandstock.com.

Extracts from *The Permanent Diaconate: Its History and Place in the Sacrament of Orders* (2007), © Kenan B. Osborne, permission granted by Publisher - Paulist Press International.

Extracts from *The Emerging Diaconate: Servant Leaders in a Servant Church* (2007) © William T. Ditewig, permission granted by Publisher - Paulist Press International.

Extracts from *The Deacon Reader* (2006) © James Keating (Editor), permission granted by Publisher - Paulist Press International.

Extracts from *Deacons and the Church* (2004) © Owen F. Cummings, permission granted by Publisher - Paulist Press International.

Extracts from *Creative Fidelity: Weighing and Interpreting Documents of the Magisterium* (1996), © Francis A. Sullivan, permission granted by Publisher - Wipf and Stock Publishers – www.wipfandstock.com.

Dr Brendan Geary FMS who generously allowed me access to the Southwark Province data from his 2007 Ushaw Study so that I could compare them with my own findings.

Fr Mark Latcovich from the Diocese of Cleveland, Ohio who granted permission for me to draw upon his 1996 research on the ministry of deacons within his diocese.

Photographs used with kind permission of Revv. Stephen Pomeroy, John Cumpsty, Andrew Philpott Anthony Clark and Roger Stone. Deacon Roger Stone's photograph was provided courtesy of *BBC South, 'Sea City'* © BBC. My thanks and sincere condolences to the family of photographer Ivan Hamilton, who kindly accompanied Deacon Stephen Pomeroy to record an entire day of ministry. Sadly, Ivan passed away shortly after the photographs were taken.

Thanks also to Professor Michael Hayes and Dr Anthony Towey, who supervised my original doctoral project at St Mary's University College, Twickenham and Fr Ashley Beck, Dean of Studies for the Permanent Diaconate in Southwark Province, for his guidance and support.

Let me also express my thanks to Bishop Crispian Hollis (Bishop Emeritus of Portsmouth), Bishop Christopher Budd (Bishop of Plymouth), Bishop Kieran Conry (Bishop of Arundel and Brighton), and Archbishop Kevin McDonald (Archbishop Emeritus of the Archdiocese of Southwark), who gave me permission to approach their deacons and affirmed my endeavours.

I am, of course, deeply indebted to the fifty three deacons who participated in the research. My aim has been to relay and interpret their testimonies with integrity and respect, and I trust that I have done so.

My thanks to Gwen and James Shaw at Matthew James Publishing for helping to bring this book to birth.

Finally, I would like to thank my family for their enthusiasm, and, in particular, my husband Tom, who has been steadfastly supportive throughout. This book is dedicated to him, with love.

Abbreviations

The documents of the Second Vatican Council used in this account are abbreviated as follows:

AA	*Apostolicam Actuositatem*	Decree on the Apostolate of Lay People
AG	*Ad Gentes Divinitus*	Decree on the Church's Missionary Activity
GS	*Gaudium et Spes*	Pastoral Constitution on the Church in the Modern World
LG	*Lumen Gentium*	Dogmatic Constitution on the Church
SC	*Sacrosanctum Concilium*	Constitution on the Sacred Liturgy

Foreword

When Jesus says to the Twelve, that "anyone who wants to become great among you must be your servant, and anyone who wants to be first among you must be your slave, just as the Son of Man came, not to be served but to serve and give his life as a ransom for many" (Mt 20:28), he is establishing the Church as a servant and serving community for the world.

Leadership in the Church has, therefore, to be characterised by the charism of service, be that leadership exercised by bishop, priest, deacon or layperson.

The precise way in which the permanent diaconate fits into that leadership pattern in the Church has been the subject of much debate – and sometimes controversy – even since the Permanent Diaconate was restored to the life of the Church by the Second Vatican Council.

Bridie Stringer in this Monograph provides us with an admirable account of that development as seen through the eyes and in the experience of permanent deacons of the Southwark Province.

All the issues have been carefully researched and explored, and from this valuable study, there emerges a vision of the permanent diaconate "as a sign of seamlessness of service in the world and church, an agent for social justice, a herald of the word and empowering servant leader", celebrated as "a valid and vital ministry and an outpouring of self-giving love."

I commend this work as a very important contribution to what has to be an on-going debate within the Church.

Bishop Crispian Hollis
Emeritus Bishop of Portsmouth

Contents

	Preface and Acknowledgements	v
	Foreword	viii
	Contents	ix
	Introduction	1
1	The Story of the Seven	5
2	The Development and Decline of the Deacon's Ministry	11
3	Why Restore the Permanent Diaconate?	21
4	What Type of Person Becomes a Permanent Deacon?	35
5	The Permanent Diaconate in the Context of the Threefold Ministry	47
6	Can a Deacon Be a Leader?	69
7	What Do Deacons Actually Do?	83
8	What Deacons Feel about their Ministry	101
9	Inviting "Theological Conversations"	111
10	Exploring the Diaconal "Microsystems"	121
11	Diaconal Formation to Support the People of God	135
12	Women's Diaconal Ministry	145
13	Summary and the Way Ahead	167
	Appendix A: Research Methodology	185
	Bibliography	193

INTRODUCTION

I have never been a huge fan of Donald Rumsfeld, the former United States Secretary of Defence but I am grateful to him for his rather tortured summary of American intelligence in the early days of the Iraq conflict:

> There are known knowns; there are things we know we know. We also know there are known unknowns; that is to say we know there are some things we do not know. But there are also unknown unknowns – the ones we don't know we don't know.[1]

This pretty much sums up my level of knowledge on the ministry of the permanent deacon when I began my doctoral research project six years ago. I knew that Roman Catholic permanent deacons were men in Holy Orders – married men mostly – that their ministry had been restored at the Second Vatican Council, that they could baptise babies, officiate at weddings, preside at funerals and lead prayers at Benediction. I also knew that there were seminarians who were ordained as "transitional" deacons about one year before becoming priests. These were celibate men who passed through their diaconal year rather like an adolescent en route to becoming an adult. I did not know that widower deacons were required to observe perpetual celibacy on the decease of their wives, a discipline which could only be dispensed in very specific and exceptional circumstances. In the "didn't know I didn't know" category was an appreciation of the deacon as a "social intermediary" i.e. someone who makes the needs of all the people known to the bishop, including the needs of non-believers. Also that he can be seen as a "minister of the threshold" – one who helps people prepare for sacramental rites of passage and is a bridge between the nave and the sanctuary in the Eucharistic celebration.

Before studying the deacon's ministry, my only experience of it was what I witnessed in various parishes in south eastern England -

compassionate and selfless ministry to those who were vulnerable and distressed. I had also been aware of parish priests who felt that their deacons were pursuing some type of pastoral hobby. I had also seen the emergence of a parish "hierarchy of credibility" which also included the deacon's wife. My intention therefore was to search beneath the surface. The former Archbishop of Canterbury Robert Runcie was attributed with the statement that the Church was like a large swimming pool, with most of the noise coming from the shallow end.[2] I wanted therefore to take my theological sonar into the deep end. This book is really my reflection on what I discovered about this ministry, the insights I derived from the stories shared by contemporary deacons about their lives and a suggested trajectory for the way ahead. As a Roman Catholic laywomen, I have had the privilege of being a type of "honest broker" for those who took part in the project. I am not formally associated with any particular diocese in the way that ordained clergy are incardinated. Nevertheless, I would like to say "thank you" for the support which the bishops of Southwark Province gave me in encouraging their deacons to take part in my work and, of course, my greatest "thank you" is to the 53 deacons themselves who participated.

What was the purpose of the project? Quite simply – to explore how the contemporary Church perceives the permanent diaconate. The lens used for this examination was the deacon's own experience – the understanding which was reflected back to him by the parish community – lay faithful and lay ministers, the parish priest, the bishop, the deacon's own family and his colleagues at work. Although this gives a limited perspective, it would have been unethical to have undertaken work which could not guarantee the anonymity of the participants. Doing case studies in parishes would have identified the deacon and his community and this carried unacceptable ethical risk. So, with those health warnings and caveats, the findings are offered to a readership which I hope will be mostly deacons and their families and those who are seeking to discern if they might have a call to the permanent diaconate. It is now just over 50 years since the opening of the Second Vatican Council at which the permanent diaconate was restored and it seems a fitting time to reflect on how this ministry has been received, how it is developing and the state of the theological questions which arise from it. Like me, most lay people have never been given any adult formation or catechesis about the deacon's ministry and are likely to be puzzled, not only by what the deacon can do or cannot do, but more importantly what the deacon is called to **be**. I would hope that after reading this account they will be able to say, "That makes a lot more sense now."

Why the title? It comes from the response given by one of the project participants when explaining how his diaconal ministry complemented the ministry of the priest and bishop, "Primarily by being married, by living in the real world where the mortgage has to be paid, the gutters cleared, the kids' vomit mopped up, the groceries bought. By standing in the dole queue. By having sex. By suffering. Very few priests and bishops have done all that. So the people can talk to you about it, in the belief that you will understand."

Over the past three years, I have taught on diaconal formation programmes and become increasingly drawn to the image of the deacon as "the minister with dirty hands". Unlike the priest, who ritually cleanses his hands at the altar before offering the Eucharistic Sacrifice in the person of Christ the Priest, the deacon stands at one remove from the altar table holding the hopes and aspirations of those on the margins and the needs of those who might otherwise be excluded from the community. He is the symbolic presence or icon of Christ the Servant, the one who washed the feet of his followers and who "came not to be served but to serve, and to give his life as a ransom for many" (Matt 20:28).

I have felt even more enthusiastic about this imagery since the election of Pope Francis I. He has urged priests too, to roll up the sleeves of their cassocks and to get their hands dirty and, in his first Chrism Mass, expressed his hope that they will be "shepherds living with the smell of the sheep."[3] I welcome the new Holy Father's simplicity and advocacy of a poor Church for the poor. Those in sacred orders and, in particular, diaconal ministry, could not be offered a stronger message of where their hearts should lie.

Endnotes

[1] US Department of Defense News Briefing 12 February 2002 http://www.defense.gov/transcripts/transcript.aspx?transcriptid=2636 accessed 18/06/2013

[2] Cited in a sermon preached in Peterhouse Chapel on the Twenty-second Sunday after Trinity, 19th November 2000, by the Rt Revd Michael Ball, OGA. http://www.pet.cam.ac.uk/chapel/ministry accessed 13/12/2010

[3] Francis I. Homily at Chrism Mass, Maundy Thursday, 28 March 2013. http://www.vatican.va/holy_father/francesco/homilies/2013/documents/papa-francesco_20130328_messa-crismale_en.html accessed 04/06/2013 – Libreria Editrice Vaticana (© Libreria Editrice Vaticana, 2013).

1 | THE STORY OF THE SEVEN

Many of us are familiar with the account in Acts 6:1-7 of seven men – Stephen, Philip, Nicanor, Prochorus, Timon, Parmenas and Nicolaus of Antioch who were selected by the community and appointed by the apostles to undertake good works which the apostles themselves were unable to perform because of the pressing need to preach the word of God. This has been interpreted traditionally as the establishment of the role of the Christian deacon as a minister of service. I must confess to have always understood this story to be one of the appropriate division of labour, with the deacons being given a social service role while the apostles carried on with the more important task of preaching. I had also seen the apostles as priestly figures in the fledgling Christian community and that they needed deacons to assist them in non-priestly tasks.

I now think it is important to realise that the apostles were **not** regarded as priests and that Jesus did not ordain the Twelve as either priests or bishops. The followers of Jesus were observant Jews and the "Jesus community" was initially a sect within Judaism. Renowned biblical scholar Raymond Brown argues that one of the reasons it is inappropriate to regard the apostles as priests is that, in the post-Ascension community, the Eucharist was not regarded as a sacrifice. He explains,

> True, there are sacrificial overtones in the traditional Eucharistic words of Jesus (the mention of the shedding of blood, the covenant motif, the "for you" theme), but this colouring was understandable because Jesus spoke these words before his bloody death. There is no proof that the Christian communities who broke the Eucharistic bread after the resurrection would have thought they were offering sacrifice.[1]

Brown does not question the legitimacy of the theology which eventually came to see the Eucharist as sacrifice (around the end of the 1st century) but he argues that the apostles would not have seen themselves as priests. The early Christians accepted the validity of the Jewish priesthood and did not seek to replace this with their own version. Even Jesus would not have qualified as a priest as he was from the tribe of Judah, not Levi. It should therefore serve as a valuable corrective to prospective deacons, or indeed their congregations, to realise that the apostles did not ordain the seven. The seven were commissioned to undertake a form of service which was not clearly specified. Ordination was a liturgical phenomenon of the post-apostolic period.

So how does this understanding clarify the role of the seven men of Acts 6 and who were the Hellenist widows? It is likely that the Hellenist widows described in Acts 6 belonged to a Diaspora community i.e. people who had been exiles elsewhere and had assimilated Greek culture and perhaps language.[2] The footnotes in the Jerusalem Bible (as used in the Lectionary readings) explain that the "Hellenists" were Jews from outside Palestine and that they had their own synagogues in Jerusalem where the scriptures were read in Greek. The "Hebrews" were Palestinian Jews and, in their synagogues, the scriptures were read in Hebrew. In the Acts account, there is a clear implication that the Hellenist widows were losing out in the charitable works of the fledgling "Jesus community". Different translations of the New Testament nuance the account in ways which can shift the emphasis from charitable work to some other form of pastoral ministry. For example, the King James translation says that "their widows (Grecians) were neglected in the daily ministration" and inserts a reference to Acts 4:35 in which is described the donation of funds to the apostles and the subsequent "distribution [was] made unto every man according as he had need". The Revised Standard Version speaks of the "daily distribution" and the apostles' reluctance to "give up preaching the word of God to serve tables". The New Jerusalem Bible speaks of "giving out food" while the recent translation of the New Testament by Fr Nicholas King SJ refers to "waiting at tables" and his footnote highlights Stephen and Philip who "turn out to be preachers, rather than officials at the soup-kitchen."³ What is not disputed is that there was a group of widows in need of care and that the community was invited to address the problem by selecting men of "good reputation, filled with the Spirit and with wisdom". As a result of the work of this group, the word of God continued to spread.

The next issue which is worthy of consideration is the actual title given to the seven. They were not called *diakonoi* (deacons). Their work was *"diakonia"*, a word which has a range of meanings and from which the term "deacon" was eventually derived. The work of scripture scholar John Collins points to a richer interpretation of the deacon's ministry than a ministry of social service. In his analysis of the use of *diakon-* words in the NT, Collins notes its use in Luke-Acts 1:8 where Peter identifies the need to replace Judas' share in this *"diakonia"* – meaning the apostolic mission to spread the Good News. In Acts 1:25, the ministry is again described as *"diakonia"* when the gathered apostles pray for discernment in nominating the new disciple. The next occurrence of the word is in Acts 6:1 in the choosing of the seven. Collins also highlights the use of the word in Acts 21:19 when used to describe Paul's missionary journey and finally, when he arrives in Jerusalem to meet with James, Paul describes what God has done among the Gentiles through his ministry/*diakonia*. Collins takes the view that the context in which Luke's audience would have understood *diakonia* was in being commissioned to carry out a sacred task. In turning his attention to the Hellenist widows, Collins surmises that their isolation could have arisen through their inability to gather in the Temple forecourts. Their needs therefore were not to be met in the provision of food but in the availability of preachers to minister to them in their own homes. This interpretation is made all the more credible by the sentence which concludes the episode i.e. that the word of God continued to spread. Collins goes so far as to offer his own version of the Acts 6 account:

> The Greek-speaking members of the community complained against those who spoke Aramaic that their housebound widows were being overlooked in the great preaching (*diakonia*) that was going on day by day in the

environs of the Temple. So the Twelve summoned the whole complement of the disciples and said 'We cannot possibly break off our public proclamation before the huge crowds in the Temple to carry out a ministry (*diakonein*) in the households of these Greek-speaking widows. Brothers, you will have to choose seven men from your own ethnic group who are fully respected, empowered by the Spirit and equipped for the task. We will then appoint them to that role that needs to be filled. That will mean that the Twelve can get on with attending to worship in the Temple and to our apostolic ministry (*diakonia*) of proclaiming the word there.'[4]

Having established that it is perhaps simplistic to read the Acts 6 account as the beginnings of a lower rank in ministerial hierarchy, it might be useful to consider other overtones in the account which would have been meaningful to Luke's audience and which can enhance our understanding of what contemporary diaconal ministry is about. For these, we must look to the Old Testament.

Recent biblical scholarship points to parallels in the calling of the seven Hellenists to Old Testament accounts of other calls to sacred service, and sees the neglect of the Hellenist widows as a breach of covenant rather than ignoring social need. Johnson in Vol 5 of *Sacra Pagina*[5] argues that, in the writing of Luke, service at table and service of the word are inextricably linked. They are not separate facets of *diakonia*. He also takes the view that the bestowal of authority on the seven results in the expansion of the mission beyond Jerusalem.[6] In other words, it is the Hellenists who hold the key to the advance of Christianity. The commissioning of the seven echoes the selection of the judges in Exodus 18:20-26 in which Jethro, the priest of Midian and father-in-law to Moses, urges him to appoint judges so that he is not worn out in settling each and every dispute among the people. In Deuteronomy 1:15-18, Moses explains to the people how they came to choose "wise and experienced men" to lead them and that their judges should administer justice, referring to him only those cases which are too difficult to adjudicate. Ben Witherington in *The Acts of the Apostles – A Socio-Rhetorical Commentary* notes a parallel between the commissioning of the seven by the laying on of hands and Moses passing on authority to Joshua in Numbers 27:15-23.[7] These overtones, far from diminishing the seven to humble table waiters, enhance their status as figures who are authorised by sacred mandate.

The connection between service to the word and to charity also has strong Old Testament roots which would not have been lost on Luke's audience. Not looking after the vulnerable, particularly widows, is a breach of the sacred covenant between God and his people, not just bad social service. Deuteronomy 24.19 speaks of leaving the forgotten sheaves for the sojourner, orphan and widow and leaving some of the olive crop and the grape harvest to be gleaned by the sojourner, orphan and widow. "You shall remember that you were a slave in the land of Egypt; therefore I command you to do this". The ministry of the word and the care of the vulnerable are of a piece – not separate functions. We only have to read James' unambiguous message in chapter 2:18 of his letter to see that there is no dichotomy between faith and the practice of good works:

> What good is it, my brothers, if a man claims to have faith but has no deeds? Can such faith save him? Suppose a brother or sister is without clothes and daily food. If one of you says to him, "Go, I wish you well; keep warm and well fed," but does nothing about his physical needs, what good is it? In the same way, faith by itself, if it is not accompanied by action, is dead. But someone will say, "You have faith; I have deeds." Show me your faith without deeds, and I will show you my faith by what I do. You believe that there is one God. Good! Even the demons believe that – and shudder.

In keeping with the theme of Old Testament commissioning, it is interesting that there were seven Hellenist leaders. This resonates with Josephus' account of his time in Galilee, recorded in his *Jewish Antiquities* of the appointment of seven judges in each of the cities, who must be "zealous in the exercise of virtue and righteousness."[8]

The only final observations to make on the selection of the seven is that the community itself chose them and presented them to the apostles. They had the endorsement of their own community. In other words, they did not perceive that they themselves were called to service, but were chosen to serve their people, and were then affirmed by the apostles. They were chosen, not for any particular talent, but because they were "of good reputation".

For personal reflection or for discussion in small groups

1. Does this fuller explanation of the Acts 6 account change the way you see the ministry of today's deacons? If so, how?
2. Who are today's Hellenist widows who are being neglected by the Church community? What can be done about it?

Endnotes

---

[1] Brown, R. 1999. *Priest and Bishop – Biblical Reflections.* Eugene, Oregon: Wipf and Stock. p.16.

[2] Mitchell, N. 1983. *Mission and Ministry- History and Theology in the Sacrament of Order.* Wilmington: Michael Glazier.

[3] *The New Testament freshly translated by Nicholas King.* 2004. Buxhall: Kevin Mayhew. p. 285.

[4] Collins, J. 2002. *Deacons and the Church.* Harrisburg: Gracewing.p. 58.

[5] Johnson, L.T. 2006. *The Acts of the Apostles- Sacra Pagina Series Vol 5.* Collegeville Minnesota: Liturgical Press. pp.105-110.

[6] Dillon, R.J. in J Fitzmyer (ed) 1991) *The New Jerome Biblical Commentary.* London: Geoffrey Chapman. p.739.

[7] Witherington, B. 1998. *The Acts of the Apostles – A Socio-Rhetorical Commentary.* Carlisle: Paternoster Press. p.248.

[8] Flavius Josephus. *Jewish Antiquities* http://www.biblestudytools.com/history/flavius-josephus/antiquities-jews/book-4/chapter-8.html?p=4 accessed 10/01/2012

2 | THE DEVELOPMENT AND DECLINE OF THE DEACON'S MINISTRY

Having established that the seven Hellenist leaders were not actually "deacons", we can now consider how the structure which we now recognise as the threefold ministry of bishop, priest and deacon actually evolved.

The early followers of Jesus are, perhaps, best described as "Christian sectarians" within Judaism rather than "Christians" per se.[1] They have been described by theologian Nathan Mitchell as a "millenarian movement" – a movement with a highly charged emotional energy, with an anticipated short life-span as heaven would soon arrive on earth, and the status quo overthrown.[2] As such, the community did not expect to need structures and codified belief systems since the "end time" was expected very soon. However, given that their chronology turned out to be incorrect, the "Jesus movement" eventually had to provide a body of written testimony and establish some kind of organisational framework to support their mission.

The leaders in the community can be readily identified in the Acts accounts. "James, the brother of the Lord" is mentioned in Acts 15:13 when he speaks for the Jerusalem community in making concessions for the pagans to become members of the community of followers: "I rule then, that instead of making things more difficult for pagans..." Peter is an acknowledged leader within the Twelve and he debates robustly with the Sanhedrin. Later in Acts, and in the Pauline letters, there are references to Phoebe, Prisca and others, suggesting that perhaps a "house Church" model was developing. Some scholars[3] surmise that that there was a different model of Church in Jerusalem, reflecting the Sanhedrin structure, to that of Antioch, where a looser organisation with prophets and teachers evolved. In short, we need to be cautious in making assumptions about the roles of bishop, deacon or priest in the early New Testament period. The "elders" mentioned in 1 Philippians 1 cannot be equated with the bishops mentioned in the letters of Ignatius of Antioch in the second century. Similarly the "*diakonoi*" described in 1 Philippians are not necessarily the same as those described by Hippolytus in the third century.

To summarise the position at the end of the apostolic period, there is little evidence to suggest that there was a single theology or structure of leadership in the early communities and, in fact, it would appear that Paul's understanding of apostleship differs from what is found in Acts. In terms of the deacon's ministry a tentative timeline for the major textual references to his role can be plotted as follows:

Biblical Texts	Approximate dates AD/CE
Acts of the Apostles	30-70/80
Letter to the Philippians	54-57
Letter to the Romans	57-58
1st Letter to Timothy	65
Letter to Titus	65

Other texts	
Didache	70-110
Clement of Rome's Epistle to the Corinthians	80
Letters of Ignatius of Antioch to the Magnesians, Trallians and Philadelphians	98-117
Justin Martyr	165
Didascalia	200+
Apostolic Tradition of Hippolytus	200+
Apostolic Constitutions	300+

It is not my intention to unpack the minute detail of the story of Christian ministry, since others have already done so. Instead, drawing upon the works of eminent scholars like Raymond Brown,

Nathan Mitchell, Henry Bettenson, Frank Hawkins and Edward Echlin, I offer a thumbnail sketch of the development of sacred ministry and, more specifically, the diaconate from the apostolic period to the 4th century.

According to Brown,[4] there were four factors which helped to force the restructuring of the community of believers in Jesus. Firstly, there were eventually more Gentile followers than Jews, possibly due to the fact that the Hellenists, or Greek-speaking believers were probably responsible for the spread of Christianity outside Judaea. Secondly, the Jerusalem community lost leadership to other centres like Rome, Antioch, Ephesus and Alexandria. Thirdly, the destruction of the Temple in Jerusalem in AD70 was interpreted by Christians as God's rejection of the Jews because of their rejection of Jesus. Fourthly, the Jewish community, in fighting to secure its own existence, began expelling its sectarian groups, including the Christians, around AD85-90.

Against this historical backdrop, we can explore the theological understandings which begin to emerge from the sacred writings of the time, specifically, the Pauline letters and the Pastoral Epistles (letters to Timothy and Titus).

The letter to the Philippians, dated around AD 54-57, opens with Paul's greeting to "all the saints in Christ Jesus, together with their presiding elders and deacons." Nothing further is offered by way of clarification of these roles. The letter to the Romans, written around the same period, commends "our sister Phoebe, a deacon[5] of the Church at Cenchreae" and refers to the help which she has given to a great many people, Paul included. It is in Chapter 3 of the first letter to Timothy that we get the equivalent of a personal profile for both the "elder" and the "deacon". Although the word "*episkopos*" is used for "elder", this does not mean "bishop" in the way we now understand this role. The character description of the deacon, with its virtue and vice lists, reflects a literary convention of the time, and commonly used by non-Christian philosophers. Again, the role cannot be assumed to be as we understand the deacon today. "Assistant" is perhaps the most appropriate way to convey its meaning.[6] The deacon's role is not well defined at this stage, but it is interesting that, like the overseer/elder, the opinion of the wider public is considered before they are appointed. The Letter to Titus which is couched rather like a Last Will and Testament lists similar qualities to those mentioned in 1 Timothy. This is relevant to the contemporary deacon in so far as the stipulation about being "married only once" is derived from these Pastoral Epistles. *The Directory for the Ministry and Life of Permanent Deacons* Chapter 3 Para 62 makes specific reference to the Pastoral Epistles in explaining that married deacons are required to embrace perpetual celibacy in the event of their wives predeceasing them. The ramifications of this, and possible exceptions, will be explored in later chapters, but at this stage, it is sufficient to refer to 1 Timothy 3:12 as the most likely genesis of what is described in the Directory as this "constant discipline of the Church in the East and West".

The *Didache*, which according to some sources[7] dates from the New Testament period, provides some pointers to the development of a wholly "Christian" ministry as distinct from the Temple Aaronic model. *Didache* Chapter 15.1 calls for the appointment of bishops and deacons "worthy of the Lord, meek men and not lovers of money, and truthful and approved for they also minister to you the ministry of the prophets and teachers". It does not specify the process by which the deacons or bishops are appointed or what differentiates them from the apostles, prophets and teachers.

The dating of the letter of Clement of Rome to the Corinthians is by no means settled among biblical scholars, with some offering a pre-AD70 date[8] and others suggesting up to 30 years later. This letter makes reference to bishops and deacons, and asserts that status and ministry are divinely ordained.

> The apostles preached to us the gospel received from Jesus Christ and Jesus Christ was God's ambassador. Christ in other words comes with a message from God and the apostles with a message from Christ. Both these orderly arrangements therefore originate from the will of God...And this was no innovation, for a long time before Scriptures had spoken about bishops and deacons; for

somewhere it says 'I will establish their overseers in observance of the law and their ministers in fidelity.'

It would appear that Clement is citing Isaiah 60:17 to bolster his argument about the authority of ministers, and, since ministry is divinely ordained, it follows that disagreement with the community leaders is tantamount to rebellion against God.[9] It is possible that Clement here is taking liberties with the complex origin of ministry and accommodating scripture to his purpose.[10]

Ignatius of Antioch's letters to the Magnesians and Trallians, dating from the early second century, are fulsome in their praise of deacons. In Magnesians Chapter 6, Ignatius sketches a trio of authority:

> The bishop is to preside in the place of God, while the presbyters are to function as the council of the Apostles and the deacons, who are most dear to me, are entrusted with the ministry of Jesus Christ, who before time began was with the Father and has at last appeared.[11]

In Chapter 2 of his letter to the Trallians,[12] Ignatius gives the deacons the title of "dispensers of the mysteries", and in Chapter 3, that they are "representing Jesus Christ", in close collaboration with the bishop and presbyters. In Chapter 10 of his letter to the Philadelphians,[13] Ignatius calls the deacon "God's ambassador", who will be sent to the Church at Antioch and Philo.

So, to summarise, there appears to be a consolidation of formal roles in ministry around the middle of the second century. As expressed in the letter to the Magnesians, the community is conceived as a divine unity and with the bishop as an individual, being subordinate to his "type" as God the Father. The deacon is a "type" of Jesus Christ and the presbyters as the Apostles.[14] In terms of diaconal duties for this period, Justin Martyr writes of deacons distributing the sacred species and taking it to absent brethren.[15] Cyprian's Epistle Chapter 12.1 says that, during times of persecution, it is permissible for deacons to be extraordinary ministers of confession and reconciliation.

...those who have received certificates from the martyrs and may be assisted by their privilege with God...without waiting for my presence, before any presbyter who might be present, or if a presbyter should not be found and death becomes imminent, before even a deacon to be able to make confession of their sins.

Some scholars take the view that the "golden age" for the deacon was the third century.[16] During this time, the deacon brought the oblations to the bishop at the Paschal Mass, and, in the Ethiopian Church, may have been a minister of anointing. The 3rd century *Didiscalia*[17] makes mention of the deacon inviting the people to reconciliation, but there is no evidence to suggest that he presided at Eucharist or routinely heard confessions. The *Didiscalia* also outlines the role of deaconesses who, because of propriety, were appointed for ministry to women.

As the third century advances, the next major feature on the landscape of Christian ministry is the *Apostolic Tradition* of Hippolytus in which the ordination ceremonies for bishops, presbyters and deacons are specified. Here, the threefold ranking of Holy Orders is clearly identified and the deacons are relegated to the third grade of office and are designated "non-priestly". The ordination rubric states that "when a deacon is ordained, the bishop alone shall lay on hands because he is not being ordained to the priesthood but to the service of the bishop". Deacons, therefore, do not occupy positions of leadership, like bishops, nor oversight, like presbyters, but are delegated tasks by the bishop. However, over the coming century, this view of the diaconate was not held universally, with some deacons presiding at the Eucharist, as attested by the canons of the Council of Arles in 314, which prohibited them from doing so thereafter. However, they could still represent the bishop at synods, assist at baptism (though not baptise), read the gospel and announce the prayers of the faithful.

During this period, there is evidence of an increased sacralisation within ministry and the beginnings of systematic disapproval of clerical marriage. The Council of Elvira (300-309) Canon 33 orders "Bishops, presbyters and deacons and all other clerics having a position in ministry ...to abstain completely from their wives and not have children. Whoever, in fact, does this shall be expelled from the dignity of the clerical state."[18] There is a wealth of scholarly debate about the subject of clerical continence and particularly with regard to the Council of Nicea (325), where it was debated but rejected by the council fathers.

The *Apostolic Constitutions*,[19] written in the latter half of the 4th century for organising Church order in Syria and Constantinople, describes Christian ministry in terms which hearken back to its Judaic forebears. The second treatise in the set of eight describes the role of the deacon in relation to that of the bishop in Judaic terms, with the bishop being regarded as a Moses figure. The bishop is also cast as the Father, with the deacon serving him as a Christ-like figure. Interestingly, the deaconess is likened to the Holy Spirit and completes the Trinitarian typology.

As mentioned earlier, the decline of the diaconate as a separate ministry is dated from around the end of the third century. One of the reasons for this was that, during the early years of Christianity, the communities of believers were located mainly in the cities of the Roman Empire, and the resident bishop, together with the deacon, could fully meet the needs of his people. As Christianity moved into the countryside, it became impossible for the bishop to attend to his widespread flock and the role of priest/presbyter developed. Since the deacon's ministry was connected directly to the bishop, the deacon did not relocate to the countryside and his role diminished to that of a transitional stage on the way to priesthood. Another explanation advanced for the decline of the permanent diaconate was the increased sacralisation of the role. The Synod of Rome, held in 595, disapproved of deacons who were neglecting the poor but were chanting psalms.[20]

In drawing this chapter to a close, I think it fair to caution against reading into the early Church models of ministry which were fixed and well-structured. Instead there was a diversity of ministry depending on geographical location and the theological understanding of local leadership. Owen Cummings in *Deacons and the Church* illustrates this diversity by offering examples of the deacons' ministry to word, liturgy and charity.[21] Lawrence of Rome, a tireless servant of the poor is cited as a minister of charity, whilst Ephrem Nisibus, a Syrian deacon from the fourth century, established a school of biblical and theological studies and could rightly be described as a "minister of the word." For the medieval period, Cummings alludes to Alcuin of York, a scholar of theology and philosophy who was involved in liturgical renewal and qualifies for the title "minister of word and of sacrament". St Francis of Assisi, with his radical poverty, shows the sacramental imagination at work, responding to God's presence everywhere. Francis could be regarded as a minister of word and sacrament who invites people to a closer sense of God's communion with them. Moving into the Reformation period, the ministry of Reginald Pole illustrates ministry to word and charity, since he was involved in both theological discourse and Church administration. Pole, incidentally, was made a cardinal whilst still a deacon and had a significant role at the Council of Trent. The Anglican deacon, Nicholas Ferrar, can be upheld as an example of ministering both word and charity since his small religious community undertook service to the poor, including a free dispensary, schooling and the distribution of food. In summing up his list of exemplary deacons, Cummings concludes:

> What may be observed through these examples from the patristic, medieval and reformation periods is that there is little uniformity in the service-in-communion of deacons down the ages. Much depended upon their gifts and how the Church used them and what the Church asked of them. We may conclude that if a historical perspective is taken, there simply is no one mould into which every deacon has to fit.[22]

It is against this backdrop that we now consider a more contemporary rationale for the restoration of the diaconate as a permanent Holy Order.

For personal reflection or for discussion in small groups

1. Which type of ministry (word, sacrament and charity) do you most associate with your parish deacon?

2. Do you think that deacons should be "recruited" in order to meet local needs e.g. chaplaincy in schools, care of refugees etc?

Endnotes
---

[1] Brown, R. 1999. *Priest and Bishop- Biblical reflections.* Eugene, Oregon: Wipf and Stock. pp.13-17.

[2] Mitchell, N. 1983. *Mission and Ministry – History and Theology in the Sacrament of Order.* Wilmington: Michael Glazier. p.105.

[3] Frend, W.H.C. 1991. *The Early Church.* Norwich: SCM. p.38.

[4] Brown, R. 1999. *Priest and Bishop- Biblical reflections.* Eugene, Oregon: Wipf and Stock. p.18.

[5] Fr Nicholas King in his translation of the New Testament notes that "some translators tend to call Phoebe a 'deaconess' but that is not what the Greek says." *The New Testament* 2006. tr. Fr Nicholas King. Buxhall: Kevin Mayhew.p.377.

[6] Fiore, B. 2003. in Harrington D. (ed) *Sacra Pagina Vol 4 The Pastoral Epistles.* Collegeville: Liturgical Press. pp 73- 83.

[7] Bettenson, H. (ed) 1963. *The Early Christian Fathers- A Selection from the Writings of the Fathers from St Clement of Rome to St Athanasius.* Translated by H. Bettenson. Oxford: Oxford University Press
See also Hawkins, F. 1992. "The Didache" in C Jones et al (eds) 1992. *The Study of Liturgy.* London: SPCK. pp.84-86.

[8] Jefford, C. 2006. *The Apostolic Fathers and The New Testament.* Peabody, Massachusetts:Hendrickson Publishers. pp.15-18.

[9] Mitchell, N, 1983. *Mission and Ministry- History and Theology in the Sacrament of Order.* Wilmington: Michael Glazier p.180.

[10] Echlin, E. 1971. *The Deacon in the Church- Past and Future.* New York: Alba House.p 15.

[11] http://www.earlychristianwritings.com/text/ignatius-magnesians-roberts.html accessed 06/02/2012

[12] http://www.earlychristianwritings.com/text/ignatius-trallians-roberts.html accessed 06/02/2012

[13] http://www.earlychristianwritings.com/text/ignatius-philadelphians-roberts.html accessed 06/02/2012

[14] Hawkins, F. 1992. "The Tradition of Ordination in the Second Century" in Jones, C., G. Wainright et al (eds) *The Study of Liturgy.* London: SPCK. pp. 84-86.

[15] http://www.earlychristianwritings.com/text/justinmartyr-firstapology.html accessed 06/02/2012

[16] Echlin, E. 1971. *The Deacon in the Church- Past and Future.* New York: Alba House. pp. 45-51.

[17] Although this document describes itself as the Teaching of the Apostles, it is really a treatise written in the third century and possibly from Syria.

[18] Council of Elvira http://www.csun.edu/~hcfll004/elvira.html accessed 22/07/2010

[19] *Apostolic Constitutions* Book 2 section 4: 29-32, http://www.newadvent.org/fathers/07152.htm accessed 10/02/2012

[20] Nowell, R. 1968. *The Ministry of Service.* London: Burns and Oates. pp.33-36.

[21] Cummings, O. F. 2004. *Deacons and the Church.* New York/Mahwah : Paulist Press. pp.53-69.

[22] Cummings, O.F., W.T. Ditewig and R.R. Gaillardetz. 2005. *Theology of the Diaconate. The State of the Question.* New York/Mahwah: Paulist Press. pp. 21-27.

3 | WHY RESTORE THE PERMANENT DIACONATE?

We closed the last chapter with a reflection on the diversity of the deacon's ministry from the first century through to the Reformation era but were also aware that for a variety of institutional and theological reasons, the diaconate eventually evolved into a transitional stage en route to priestly Holy Orders. In this chapter, we explore the reasons why the Council Fathers at Vatican II decided to restore the diaconate as a permanent Holy Order.

The decision of the Council Fathers was the culmination of a long period of reflection and discernment starting in late 19th century Germany.[1] Here, there was a perception that priests were somewhat remote from the daily lives of their people and that a married diaconate might counterbalance this tendency. The alternative was to permit priests to marry. This view was also held elsewhere in Europe, but it was the German experience which was to be the most influential. There were arguably four factors which set the scene for the serious consideration of the matter. Firstly the German experience of charitable outreach which was undertaken by *Caritas* at the end of WW1. This was followed by the "Dachau experience", in which imprisoned priests in Nazi Germany reflected on what type of Church would emerge from the aftermath of the Second World War, and what type of pastoral provision could be offered. The third factor was a consideration that a local ordained ministry in mission territories would support communities in the absence of the priest. Fourthly, Pope Pius XII in his Apostolic Constitution *Sacramentum Ordinis* (1947) confirmed that the diaconate was part of a threefold ministry of order, dispelling doubts that only the priestly order was sacramental. In his address to the Second World Congress of the Lay Apostolate in Rome on 5

October 1957, he alluded to the possibility of a restoration of the permanent diaconate:

> We know that thought is being given at present to the introduction of a diaconate conceived as an ecclesiastical office independent of the priesthood. Today, at least, the idea is not yet ready for application.[2]

The possibility raised by Pope Pius finally came to fruition with the promulgation of the *Dogmatic Constitution on the Church* on 21 November 1964. This document, generally known by its opening words, *Lumen Gentium,* was one of the most significant documents of the Council and was accorded the highest level of authority i.e. dogmatic. Commentators are generally in agreement that this was the central document of the Council and one which presented the fullest and most detailed understanding of the Church ever developed by a council.[3] It defined the Church, in Christ, to be "a sacrament – a sign and instrument ...of communion with God and of the unity for the entire human race." It also named the Church as "People of God" and a "Pilgrim People", not yet perfected but journeying until "in the end, it shall be manifested in full light".[4] This was in direct contrast to the Church's earlier self-understanding, expressed as "a perfect society". It is worth comparing the content and tone of Pope Pius IX's 1874 encyclical *On the Church in Austria (Vix dum a Nobis)*[5] with that of *Lumen Gentium*. In the former document in a section titled "Ecclesiastical Authority" we have the following:

> God equipped the Church with the divine gifts of an infallible teaching authority for handing on sacred doctrine and of a most holy priesthood. He also equipped it with the power to pass laws, exercise judgments, and employ salutary coercion in all matters which pertain to the kingdom of God on earth.
>
> This supernatural power of ecclesiastical rule is different from and independent from political authority. For this reason the kingdom of God on earth is a perfect society, which is held together and governed by its own laws and its own rights. Its own overseers keep watch in order to

account for souls, not to the rulers of civil society, but to the chief Pastor, Jesus Christ, from whom come pastors and teachers subject to no earthly authority in carrying out the task of salvation. Wherefore, just as the duty to rule belongs to the holy bishops, so all the faithful, as the Apostle points out, are bound to obey and be subject to them; therefore, Catholic people have a right not to be impeded in this divinely imposed duty of following the doctrine, discipline, and laws of the Church.

The historical context of the encyclical is the impending prospect of the Church being made subject to the laws of the Austrian Assembly. In order to defend its position, Pope Pius IX has deployed a theological argument using apostolic authority to insulate the Church from the need to engage with civil authority. It argues from a position of infallible teaching, authority and governance which is not accountable to civil laws as it is, in itself, "a perfect society".[6] By contrast, *Lumen Gentium*, in a section titled "The Pilgrim Church" holds that:

> The Church, to which we are all called in Christ Jesus, and in which by the grace of God we attain holiness, will receive its perfection only in the glory of heaven when the time for renewal of all things will have come (Acts 3:21) (LG48).

Commentators on the Council make frequent mention of the fact that the ordering of the chapters of *Lumen Gentium* was revised so that the chapter entitled "People of God" preceded the chapter on the "Church as hierarchical." The constitution also dramatically redrew the ecclesiastical landscape by declaring the episcopacy "the fullness of the Sacrament of Orders" (LG26), with priests defined as the "prudent co-operators of the episcopal college and its support and instrument, called to the service of the People of God" and who "constitute together with their bishop, one presbyterate, though dedicated to a variety of duties"(LG 26). The term "fullness of orders" was not elaborated and therefore became the cause of confusion of priestly identity which pertains to the present day. LG29 describes the deacons, who are situated at "a lower level of hierarchy" and "who receive the imposition of hands, not for priesthood but for service." Their role is undertaken "in communion with the bishop and his presbyterate, in the service of the liturgy, the word and charity." The deacon's specific tasks are:

- To administer Baptism solemnly
- To reserve and distribute the Eucharist
- To assist at and to bless marriages in the name of the Church
- To take Viaticum to the dying
- To read sacred scripture to the faithful
- To instruct and exhort the people
- To preside over the worship and the prayer of the faithful
- To administer sacramentals
- To officiate at funeral and burial services

The constitution justifies the restoration of the diaconate as a permanent clerical state on the grounds that "the laws and customs of the Latin Church in force today in many areas render it difficult to fulfil the functions" listed above. This assertion is worth testing against the backdrop of a Vatican II theology of the laity which celebrates their call to a threefold priesthood to proclaim, sanctify and lead. It could be argued that the Church in "reading the signs of the times" (GS4) could have facilitated the development of lay ecclesial ministry over against the restoration of the moribund order of the permanent diaconate. To counterbalance this however, the sacrament of Holy Order as an instrument of grace should not be overlooked.

The Council's *Decree on the Church's Missionary Activity* (*Ad Gentes*), promulgated in 1965, endorsed the diaconate's restoration, but with the caveat: "wherever it appears opportune to episcopal conferences" (AG16). In other words, bishops could themselves decide whether or not to restore the permanent diaconate, and within the Roman Catholic Church in England and Wales, the Diocese of Salford continues not to have permanent deacons.

The rationale suggested for its restoration was that it would help those men who were already carrying out the ministry of the diaconate – preaching the word of God as catechists, governing scattered Christian communities in the name of the bishop or parish priest, or exercising charity in the performance of social or charitable works. It was felt that these men would be strengthened with the grace of Holy Orders through the imposition of hands, which had come down the ages from the apostles. As a result "they would be more closely bound to the altar and their ministry would be made more fruitful through the sacramental grace of the diaconate" (AG16).

The restoration was to be considered initially for a five year period, and during this time, candidates should not be a financial liability on their diocese – it should be unpaid voluntary work.

Reasons for restoring the Permanent Diaconate

The *Basic Norms for the Permanent Diaconate*[7] lists three reasons for its restoration:

- Enriching the Church
- Strengthening those already exercising many functions of the diaconate
- The provision of sacred ministry in the event of the shortage of clergy

Enriching the church

Looking back to the Council after an interval of fifty years, it is easy to imagine fraternal and gracious debates among the Council fathers. But rather like the account in Acts 2 of a loving and peaceful early community of believers, this vision of conciliar solidarity is somewhat optimistic. The debates were much more robust and some of the bishops were strongly opposed to the restoration of the diaconate as a permanent Holy Order. Xavier Rynne's account of the Council[8] highlights Cardinal Spellman's reservations, which he expressed in his speech to the Council on 4 October 1963, a year before the promulgation of *Lumen Gentium:* "God exercises his providence over the Church, according to its present conditions. It must be decided whether it is better to by-pass the divine will and have fewer priests, along with permanent deacons or more priests without them." Later, he added, "The reason I am against it is because it is unnecessary." The cardinal also felt that married men who were aspirant deacons could not be educated in the same institution as celibate priests and that, if a married diaconate became the norm, the number of priestly vocations would decline "for youth was always prone to choose the easier way." Countering Spellman's discomfiture, Cardinal Suenens from Belgium felt that the restoration of the permanent diaconate would give greater prominence to the diaconate overall and make it possible for large segments of the faithful to "enjoy in greater abundance, the gifts that flow from the supernatural riches of the Church". In his account of the debates, Gérard Philips notes that the discussions were all the livelier for being focused around practical questions, without paying sufficient attention to the theological aspects of the problem. Relegating some priestly tasks to lay people, or giving them to those in minor orders, as suggested by the conservative Cardinal Ottaviani were challenged by Suenens, "Why should sacramental grace be denied to those to whom a charge of hierarchy is entrusted? The sacraments are there to be used and we let the ritual stand in the way!"[9] Rather than performing work which laymen could do, Suenens envisaged that the work entrusted to deacons would flow from the order that they had received. According to Rynne, many of the Council fathers from mission areas saw advantages in being able to deploy deacons as leaders for communities which would otherwise not benefit from the care of a resident pastor. However, some of the bishops who voted in favour were happy to advocate deacons for their less advantaged fellow-bishops, but did not want them for themselves. Some members of the African episcopate, for example, supported their Latin-American brother bishops in voting for the restoration but did not see the need for it in their own territories. The African model of local leadership, in the form of lay catechists, still prevails and it is particularly noteworthy that the territories within which the permanent diaconate flourished, and continues to do so, are the USA and Europe. According to the 2012 Annual Directory of the Holy See (*Annuario Pontificio*) by the end of 2010, there were 39,564 permanent deacons throughout the world, an increase of 3.7% from 38,155 the previous year. 64% of deacons are North Americans and 33% European.

The restoration of the permanent diaconate, coupled with the uncertainty about priestly identity and the vexed question of priestly celibacy, which *Lumen Gentium* had engendered were the subject of further discussions in the 1971 Synod of Bishops on Ministry. Belgian theologian, Edward Schillebeeckx's account of the synod[10] cites prevailing doubts about the specificity or distinctiveness of the official priesthood compared with the universal priesthood of all believers. He also notes the synodal discussions on the possibility of instituting priesthood for a specific period and the theological ambiguity resulting from having lay leaders in faith communities without official mandate of Holy Orders. In seeking to settle these questions, it might be argued that the restoration of the permanent diaconate and, in particular, approval for a married diaconate, was an expedient "get out" clause for an institutional conundrum which could not easily be solved.

Strengthening those already exercising many functions of the diaconate

The argument poses some difficulty when placed under scrutiny. The deacon's duties as listed in the Basic Norms were not undertaken by lay people in the Roman Catholic Church in the pre-Vatican II period. It could possibly be argued that a range of priestly duties deemed appropriate for those in the lower diaconal order were simply shunted from priest to deacon in order to assign the latter a sacramental role and to shore up the presbyteral priesthood placed under pressure by a shortage of manpower. The growth in lay liturgical ministry could not of course have been foreseen, but having enjoined lay people to appropriate their full baptismal responsibilities to word, sacrament and service, it is now possible that diaconal orders may simply frustrate the aspirations of the laity to serve their communities more faithfully.

There are also of course fundamental issues of equality. The role of women in the service of the Church in liturgical and pastoral ministry cannot be easily dismissed. As administrators of parishes and other Church bodies, they are clearly ministers of service. As catechists, readers, scripture scholars and theologians they are ministers of the word. They are also Extraordinary Ministers of Holy Communion and Baptism. The denial of Holy Orders for women continues to be a contentious issue and will be explored further in Chapter 12.

The provision of sacred ministry in the event of the shortage of clergy

This third objective pre-supposes that unmet pastoral need resulting from a shortage of priests can be addressed by the ministry of deacons. As already noted, in Western Europe and the USA where priestly vocations are in decline, there is a steady increase in candidacy for the permanent diaconate. However, this increase clearly does not address the basic sacramental deficits in the provision of Eucharist, Reconciliation and Sacrament of the Sick. Lay faithful may be commissioned as Extraordinary Ministers to baptise and officiate at weddings and funerals. They also routinely provide high quality pastoral leadership and catechesis – all functions which are detailed as within the remit of the permanent deacon. Presiding at the Eucharist and administering the Sacraments of the Sick and Reconciliation are outside the remit of both deacons and lay people and are, arguably, the most fundamental sacramental needs after Baptism. In this regard, the restoration of the permanent diaconate could never have been envisaged as a solution to these sacramental deficits.

American theologian Kenan Osborne's account of the development of the Sacrament of the Sick provides refreshing insight into how the current needs of the frail and housebound might be addressed by diaconal service. He reminds us that the connection between sacramental healing and the forgiveness of sin was a theological development of the Scholastic period. In the early Church (up to AD 313) oils blessed by the *episkopos* were used by lay people to anoint the sick. In the period up to AD 751, he cites many examples where this practice prevailed, including Innocent I's letter to Bishop Decentus of Gubbio, which refers to the holy oil which is "licitly anointed not only by priests but by all Christians for their own needs and for the needs of others".[11] Eligible for this anointing were those of any age who suffered any illness, including mental incapacity. It was only in the Scholastic period that the priest alone was authorised to anoint and small children and those who were mentally "handicapped" were ineligible for ministry in this way. Dying became the main focus for the Sacrament of the Sick and the major effect was the forgiveness of sin rather than healing. Osborne takes the view that the Scholastic interpretation of the Sacrament of the Sick impacts on contemporary understanding and that perhaps it should be revisited in the light of contemporary practice. He summarises the issue as follows:

> The theology of sacraments was a theological interpretation of the praxis of the time. The theologians theologized on the basis of the praxis. Now we recognise the historical relativity of the praxis and hence the theology. The bishops and theologians at Trent had no idea of the history behind the sacramental rite of anointing. The Tridentine theological presentation was based on their contemporary praxis i.e. an unreflected position, historically speaking.[12]

What Osborne appears to be saying is that, by returning to the origins of sacramental anointing of the sick and detaching these from the Sacrament of Reconciliation, it may be possible to provide diaconal ministry to the sick and housebound within a recast Sacrament for the Sick. This provision could also perhaps be considered as one of "extraordinary lay ministry" in much the same way as Extraordinary Ministers of the Eucharist bring the sacred species and break open the word to those unable to attend the Eucharistic assembly because of illness and other frailty. Clearly, this still does not address the problem of ministering the Sacrament of Reconciliation, but a revised rite of Sacrament of the Sick could offer a graced encounter which is currently not possible for many ill and frail members of the Church. Osborne suggests that when the institutional Church does not address glaring pastoral need, then its *diakonia* is compromised.

Role of the laity

The role of the laity in the work of the Kingdom was perhaps one of the most significant positive outcomes from the Second Vatican Council. Lay people, the majority of Church membership, who had previously been defined in terms of what they were **not** i.e. non-ordained, were now encouraged to become fully active, conscious and participative[13] in the Church body. *Lumen Gentium* elaborated on this by distinguishing the common priesthood of all believers and the ordained hierarchical priesthood of Sacred Orders.

> Though they differ essentially and not only in degree, the common priesthood of the faithful and the ministerial or hierarchical priesthood are none the less interrelated; each in its own way shares in the one priesthood of Christ. The ministerial priest, by the sacred power that he has, forms and governs the priestly people: in the person of Christ he brings about the Eucharistic sacrifice and offers it to God in the name of the people. The faithful indeed by virtue of their royal priesthood, share in the offering of the Eucharist. They exercise that priesthood too by the reception of the sacraments, by prayer and thanksgiving, by the witness of a holy life, self-denial and active charity (LG10).

This articulation of the rights and responsibilities of all believers, based upon their baptismal calling, was further elaborated in the *Constitution on the Apostolate of Lay People* (*Apostolicam Actuositatem*) promulgated in 1965. In short, these constitutions were the foundation stones upon which were built the commissioned roles and responsibilities now regarded as normative within the life of the Church – readers, cantors, Extraordinary Ministers of Holy Communion and membership of pastoral councils. The effect of this development on Holy Orders has already been noted, as many members of the lay faithful now participate in areas of ecclesial ministry which were previously the exclusive domain of those in Holy Orders e.g. sacramental preparation programmes for baptism and marriage, pastoral visiting of parishioners and studies in the "sacred sciences".

The wider context – church in the world

These developments, however, cannot be explored as isolated Church phenomena. In society at large, postmodernism has challenged the authority of the Church as an arbiter of moral and social issues. For many, the institutional Church appears to witness the debates on major social issues rather than participate in them. Its messages on the global economy, oppression of developing nations, multiculturalism and ecology appear at times reactive rather than proactive and kerygmatic. Its support for the rights and equality of women can at times appear perplexing when set against the background of its own ordered institution.

Ronald Rolheiser[14] summarises the dilemma of being in the world but not of it and that secularity itself evolves and develops. He says:

> The secular world is not a moral cesspool within which faith's task is to convert the godless. The secular world is still a world loved by God and a world with much moral and spiritual strength. In the name of faith, we are called to love that world. …Like *Gaudium et Spes*… we are being evangelised by the culture even as we are evangelising it.

The nature of Church authority is itself a complex theological mystery. Biblical scholar John L. McKenzie[15] asserts that authority is indestructible and incorruptible in the Church but that the concrete forms in which the authority appears do not share this incorruptibility. He takes the view that the Church has not developed models of authority which parallel the development of legitimate state systems. Instead it has adhered to forms which rather reflect the regime of absolute rulers. He poses a Jeffersonian model in which the consent of the governed is the legitimate mandate for those who govern and contends that the Christian life cannot be conceived in Biblical terms as a life of submission and obedience but as something else in which both have a place. For McKenzie, the centre of gravity is the enduring life of Christ, not the authority of the Church as institution. He alludes to Matthew 20:20-28, Mark 10:35-45 and Luke 22:28-27 as the simple manifesto for *"diakonos"* – the word itself, translated in its New Testament context, not as "servant" but "child", "lackey" or "slave."[16] McKenzie notes that Jesus could have applied any metaphor for the twelve e.g. that of scribe. Instead, he used a metaphor to show that the lives of his followers were to be expended totally in the service of others. They were to assume the status of non-people i.e. the child or the slave. In seeking to define the authority of Jesus, McKenzie sees no tension between his *diakonia*, his power and his authority. His divinely-given authority is not transferred to his followers but, by virtue of this authority, he sends his followers forth to make disciples of all people. He commissioned the Church to find ways and structures to bring about an entirely new community of love.[17]

It is within this complex theological, philosophical and ecclesiological dynamic that we situate the ministry of the post-Vatican II permanent deacon. What is his calling? How does he name his giftedness? How does he perceive his threefold ministry in relation to his bishop, his presbyters and his faith-sharing community? How does he witness in the secular world to his calling and bring to his calling the richness of his family and professional life? How does he assist the community to fully pour itself out in the service of the Kingdom without lording over it? As McKenzie points out, "one of the ways the Church suffers is from poverty of the kind of person who can bear authority in the Church worthily. Jesus himself sought twelve and found only eleven."[18]

For personal reflection or for discussion in small groups

1. In the light of the development of lay ministry after the Second Vatican Council, how can the deacon's ministry assist the lay faithful to respond to their calling as baptised Christians?
2. Thinking of your own experience in the parish, is there any tension in those areas of ministry which can be undertaken by both deacons and lay people e.g. catechesis? If so, how can these be resolved?

Endnotes

---

[1] Ditewig, W.T. 2007. *The Emerging Diaconate*. New York: Paulist Press. pp.95-102.

[2] Pius XII 1957. *Guiding Principles of the Lay Apostolate*. http://www.papalencyclicals.net/Pius12/P12LAYAP.HTM accessed 06/02/2012.

[3] Jamison, C., D. Lundy, and L. Poole. 1995. *To Live is to Change – A Way of Reading Vatican II*. Chelmsford: Rejoice Publications.

[4] *Lumen Gentium* abbreviated to LG. (LG8)

[5] Pope Pius IX. 1874. *On the Church in Austria*. http://www.papalencyclicals.net/Pius09/p9vixdum.htm accessed 06/02/2012.

[6] See also Pope Pius XI's 1925 Encyclical *Quas Primas* 31 in which the Church "has a natural and inalienable right to perfect freedom and immunity from the power of the state" http://www.vatican.va/holy_father/pius_xi/encyclicals/ documents/hf_p-xi_enc_11121925_quas-primas_en.html accessed 06/02/2012 – Libreria Editrice Vaticana (© Libreria Editrice Vaticana, 2013).

[7] Congregation for the Clergy. 1998. *Basic Norms for the Formation of Permanent Deacons*. London: CTS p.13.

[8] Rynne, X. 1999. *Vatican Council II*. New York: Orbis Books p. 188.

[9] Philips, G. 1966 in Vorgrimler, H. (ed) *Commentary on the Documents of Vatican II*. English translation by K. Smyth, L. Adolphus and R. Strachan. London: Burnes and Oates: Herder and Herder. pp.105-137

[10] Schillebeeckx, E. 1980. *Ministry – A Case for Change*. London: SCM. p.140.

[11] Osborne, K. 2006. *The Permanent Diaconate – its History and Place in the Sacrament of Orders*. New York: Paulist Press p.18.

[12] Ibid p.189.

[13] *The Constitution on the Sacred Liturgy* (*Sacrosanctum Concilium*) states that "it is very much the wish of the Church that all the faithful should be led to take that full, conscious and active part in liturgical celebrations which is demanded by the very nature of the liturgy and to which the Christian people 'a chosen race, a royal priesthood, a holy nation, a redeemed people' (1Peter 2: 9, 4-5) have a right and to which they are bound by reason of their Baptism"(SC14).

[14] Rolheiser, R. 2006. *Secularity and the Gospel*. New York: Crossroad. p.46.

[15] McKenzie. J.L. 1985. *Authority in the Church*. London: Geoffrey Chapman. p13.

[16] Collins, J. 2002. *Deacons and the Church*. Harrisburg: Gracewing. pp. 32-45.
[17] McKenzie. J.L. 1985. *Authority in the Church*. London: Geoffrey Chapman p.31.
[18] Ibid p.177.

4 | WHAT TYPE OF PERSON BECOMES A PERMANENT DEACON?

This chapter will focus on some of the questions which were asked of the deacons taking part in the Southwark Province research project. The project researcher invited all 172 deacons of Southwark Province to complete a questionnaire about their call to ministry, their formation and subsequent experience in their parishes. The purpose of the exercise was to determine how the Church community perceives the ministry of deacons. The lens through which this was explored was, of course, that of the deacon – in other words, what understanding of the permanent diaconate emerges from the interactions which occur between the deacon and lay people, lay ministers, priest and bishops? The overall research question was couched as: "What is the ecclesial understanding of the role of the permanent diaconate in the contemporary Roman Catholic Church in England and Wales, with specific reference to Southwark Province?" For those who are interested in the rigour of the research process, the research methodology is detailed in Appendix A.

Southwark Province consists of Southwark Archdiocese and the dioceses of Portsmouth, Plymouth and Arundel and Brighton. The rationale for choosing this area was that it provided a mix of urban, rural, and metropolitan communities, and that findings could perhaps be extrapolated elsewhere. Having said that, it was never the intention to make statistical claims from the findings, but instead to give an account of the deacons' stories and to use their own words where possible. The questionnaires invited the deacons to describe their experiences rather than to tick boxes or to score results against pre-determined scales. 53 deacons responded (30.8%) – a rich return, generously offered and gratefully received. The return rate per diocese was as follows:

Diocese	No. of deacons in diocese	No. of respondents	Respondents as % of deacons in the diocese	% of total respondents
Arundel & Brighton	34	10	29.41	18
Plymouth	24	7	29.16	13
Portsmouth	38	13	34.21	25
Southwark	76	23	30.26	43
TOTAL	172	53	30.81	99

Age of respondents

The age profile of the 53 respondents was as follows:

Ages	40-44	45-49	50-54	55-59	60-64	65-69	70-74	75-97	80+
No	3	2	4	10	9	5	10	4	6

This demographic reflects the canonical requirements of permanent deacons to be men of at least 35 years, settled in their family lives and to be financially independent. In the case of the Southwark Province respondents, 58.5% were retired or semi-retired.

Marital status

In terms of their marital status, the majority of respondents were married (85%), with an additional 9.4% now widowers, and the remaining 5% single. The ethnic profile of the group was mainly white British or Irish. Some offered variations not generally found in census returns, like "European Irish", "White British (Yorkshire)", and "White European". Again, it was important not to seek to pigeon-hole people but to allow them to name their own identities. In terms of faith background, 35.8% of respondents were not "cradle Catholics", having come from other Christian denominations, mainly Anglicanism. Two were former Methodists, and one from each of the Church of Scotland, Church in Wales and a

"Catholic/Christian Fellowship community". 19% of respondents had felt drawn to sacred ministry at an earlier stage in their lives. Some had explored priesthood within the Anglican Church before their conversion to Roman Catholicism, whilst others had tested vocations to the priesthood, but found that they did not have the gift of celibacy. In considering this data, caution should be applied to any interpretation which suggests that deacons are really "frustrated priests" and that, were the discipline of celibacy to be removed from priesthood these former seminarians would have preferred to seek priestly ordination rather than the permanent diaconate. Having acknowledged this, one of the cohort, now widowed, is in priestly formation.

Professional lives

With regard to their professional lives, the deacons of the project followed a wide range of careers including horticulture, agriculture, chartered engineering, industrial chemistry, university lecturing, accountancy, civil service, clinical consultancy in the health service, technical roles in IT and officers in local government. It was clear that this diversity of experience and rootedness in secular society lends credibility and empathy to the ministry of the contemporary deacon. It is interesting to contrast this range of professional backgrounds with those suggested by Nowell in *The Ministry of Service* published in 1968. Here, Nowell surmised that deacons would probably emerge from the "caring" professions, particularly social work. He went so far as to caution against the recruitment of men "wielding secular authority", citing prison officers and those working in offenders institutions as unsuitable for diaconal ministry.[1] To the contemporary mature Catholic, this seems a rather narrow reading of both authority and diaconal service. Nowell seems to suggest that secular authority manifests itself only in hierarchical autocracies and also that there are some legitimate professions which are fundamentally at odds with the universal call to holiness and service to the People of God. A more nuanced reading of authority would today include "soft" skills of empowering leadership, coaching and mentoring. To return specifically to Nowell's example, however, the presence of deacons in custodial settings in roles other than chaplaincy might well challenge and ameliorate some of the abusive institutional practices which attract public alarm. Within the Southwark Province group of deacons, one respondent's professional role involved him in work with personality- disordered offenders and he expressed his desire to use these professional skills more widely in his diaconal ministry. Another respondent in addressing the question "Are your work colleagues aware that you are in Roman Catholic Holy Orders?" replied: "The Chief Executive does; my manager is aware that I'm ordained and this is included in some personal details on the intranet, without specifying the denomination. Nowadays, this is a delicate matter, particularly for a Christian, more still for an RC Christian who is ordained." One of the group noted that it was his Roman Catholic colleagues in particular who viewed his ministry in a negative light, and for another, there was concern in the senior management of his company because "they didn't want a 'Holy Joe'". In contrast, however, another found that his ministry was a sign to colleagues that he could be trusted with their confidences and provide emotional support in crises. Another felt very affirmed when a colleague suggested to another who was having problems: "Do you want to talk to our deacon?"

The backgrounds of the group reflected the tertiary level educational requirements of their professions, whilst theological literacy was achieved in a variety of ways depending on when their formation programmes had been undertaken. The data for this question were arranged into 3 cohorts – the 70/80s, the 90s, the 00s. The earliest candidates in the 70s had received a very personalised formation, with some enjoying an almost tutelage arrangement with their bishops. One such candidate had met with a priest-tutor weekly and all his written work sent to the bishop. He would then meet quarterly for an afternoon and evening session with the bishop and the work discussed. This was supplemented by courses at Hawkstone Hall and the Grail. The 1980s cohort, whilst having monthly lectures in moral and dogmatic theology, Church history and scripture, had a somewhat less personalised formation and there was no formal qualification. One of the group described it as "very much a guinea pig operation". By the 1990s however, more formal courses and opportunities for accredited qualifications were available. Although the Wonersh Seminary formation programme, undertaken over 3 years, delivered no formal qualification, some of the group from this period gained other relevant accreditations – Catholic Certificate for Religious Education (CCRE), Diploma in Pastoral Theology, BA degrees in Divinity and Catholic Theology. By the 2000s, Wonersh was offering an NVQ Level 3 in Pastoral Ministry, although again, like the 1990s group, some of the students gained theological degrees and diplomas in other institutions. Current formation at Wonersh now includes a Foundation Degree of Arts (FdA) in Pastoral Ministry which is available under the auspices of St Mary's University College, Strawberry Hill. This 3-year course can be supplemented by further study to progress to a BA (Hons) degree in Theology. This increasingly academic steer may be problematical for some who would aspire to the permanent diaconate. They may perhaps perceive their learning to be more intuitive or practical. However, it should be acknowledged that a ministry which puts the proclamation of the word at its heart requires a rigorous scriptural formation in order to be truly effective. Leadership in pastoral ministry also requires a systematic discipline in order to deliver appropriate care and support. As formally mandated ministers of the institutional Church, who are sacramentally ordained and canonically accountable, the discipline of academic theology now seems to be an essential tool in the deacon's ecclesiastical toolbox.

Other qualifications gained by the group overall included philosophy, politics, computer science etc in order to support their professional lives. Perhaps the most versatile range of accomplishments came from the respondent who listed: Diploma in Pastoral Theology, Catholic Teaching Certificate, RCIA, Marriage Auditor, diocesan training days for clergy, deacon training days, chain saw operator and tractor driver!

Voluntary work undertaken in the last 10 years

The deacons were invited to detail any voluntary work they had undertaken in the previous 10 years. The rationale for this question was that for many, the defining charism of the deacon is in works of charity. The *General Norms for the Permanent Diaconate*[2] underscore this value:

> ...no-one can be called to the diaconate unless he has gained the high regard of clergy and the faithful by a long example of truly Christian life, by his unexceptionable conduct and by his ready disposition to be of service (General Norms iii.12).

The respondents delivered an abundant harvest in voluntary work – from parish-based administration to chaplaincy roles in prisons and hospitals. Catholic charitable organisations like St Vincent de Paul, CAFOD, pilgrimage co-ordination and Marriage Care were just some of the beneficiaries of the group. Secular charities devoted to the care of the elderly, the homeless, those with learning difficulties and residents in sheltered accommodation also featured in the deacons' repertoire of voluntary service. One of the most striking responses to this question came from a deacon who had "stood as security for an asylum seeker."

One response was initially perplexing – 'emptying Sooties for RNIB'. I then remembered the *Royal National Institute for the Blind* collecting boxes which featured the beloved TV puppet, Sooty. The deacon was a volunteer acting on behalf of RNIB. In terms of civic responsibilities, the group also listed roles in political parties, school governorships, local tourism bodies and some sports organisations. Of the three ordained orders, only the deacon is permitted to hold an official role in civic life and hold a secular profession.

How long a deacon?

The Southwark Province respondents had accumulated some 680 years of service in ordained ministry. The following table shows the spread of experience and it is interesting that 6 deacons in the group have served for more than 26 years.

< 3 yrs	3-5 yrs	6-10 yrs	11-15 yrs	16-20 yrs	21-15 yrs	> 26 yrs
4	9	11	10	9	4	6

31 deacons (58.5%) declared themselves to be now retired or semi-retired. Two indicated that they taken early retirement in order to focus on their diaconal ministry. Two more had reduced their working time whilst 3 had entirely changed their careers. One noted that his career had been curtailed as a result of his call to ministry and another felt that there was a "jealousy" in the workplace about the extent of his commitment to ministry. One member of the group had retired to train for the priesthood. In summing up these snippets of reflection on the professional lives of the 53, it seems appropriate to quote Kasper who acknowledged the diaconate as a calling of humility and willingness to serve, calling it a "downwardly mobile career."[3]

Formation /training and ongoing support/development

The formation of the group had been undertaken in several establishments, depending upon their diocese. 39 had attended Wonersh Seminary, whilst 6 had attended the Carmelite House in Allington Castle. The remainder had attended courses in Maryvale (Birmingham Archdiocese), Park Place Pastoral Centre (Portsmouth Diocese) and other unspecified venues in Clifton and Plymouth dioceses. St John's Seminary in Wonersh currently provides diaconal formation for the dioceses of Arundel and Brighton, Portsmouth, Plymouth, Brentwood, Cardiff, East Anglia, Northampton, Westminster and Southwark.

What surprised you most in the training/formation?

The deacons were then asked what had surprised them most in their training/formation. The deacons from the 1970s were, of course, the trailblazers for this new exciting ministry and nothing surprised them. As one expressed it "Nothing (surprised me) – except that the archbishop had actually accepted me for training!" Another felt "overjoyed that at last, it was beginning to happen." One reservation was expressed about the lack of understanding of collaborative ministry, not only in the 1970s, but continuing to the present day.

The deacons ordained in the 1980 re-echoed some of these positive comments and spoke of the relaxed atmosphere, good team spirit and the high standard of the lectures. For one, the informality of the sessions was a pleasant surprise. More negative observations included the lack of practical input and "no proper structure or thought for the training. Obviously not in-depth as for priesthood but again how much less! It appeared rather hit and miss – let's try it out and see how it goes." This was echoed by another respondent who was "a little perturbed by the superficiality of some modules e.g. New Testament study. As a professional, I remember how unequal was the quality of tutors/lecturers from inspirational to abysmal." For another, the deficiencies in the formal moral theology formation were remedied via his tutor who was a "capable moral theologian." A further negative comment was made about the "extraordinary lack of hospitality from the resident priestly student body."

Like their brother deacons of the previous decade, the 1990s cohort expressed surprise at the lack of practical aspects, including homily practice and care of the dying and bereaved. One mentioned "how very little it was based on the reality of being a person of more mature years called to the ordained ministry", whilst another found it time-consuming and the number one priority after the family. Four respondents found nothing in the programme which surprised them, whilst others expressed their enjoyment of finding they could cope with the reading and studies, and found no clash with their working lives. In terms of the quality of the programme content, one described it as "sketchy" and lacking the depth needed for teaching and preaching, whilst another found it "not that well worked out but maybe that was to do with diocesan teething troubles" and added that "things seemed to have improved now." Two additional strands emerged from this group – "the conservative attitude of much of the formation" although this was not elaborated further, and the fact that, according to one respondent, "many candidates held opinions contrary to the Church's teaching."

The responses to this question from the 2000s group highlighted the fellowship of the group and the inclusion of wives as positive aspects. Others mentioned the formation of the person as opposed to the academic orientation of the programme to be very appealing. One noted that "some of my fellow candidates who began the programme had little or no formal qualifications but I would now count as very able deacons." From my own experience as a member of the teaching team for deacons in formation, the pastoral ministry which lies at the heart of the formation process is striking and transformative. On each formation day, members of the student body undertake the duties of hospitality at coffee breaks and mealtimes. Designated members of the group serve at the mealtime table and make sure that the dishes are cleared. The gracious attentiveness to this task is almost Benedictine in its execution. Benedict in describing the qualifications of the monastery cellarer in Chapter 31 of his monastic rule says:

> He will regard all utensils and goods of the monastery as sacred vessels of the altar, aware that nothing is to be neglected.[4]

This aspect of the Wonersh experience is as striking as the devout liturgical observance during Mass and the Divine Office.

In drawing this section to a close I am aware that in the current financial climate and the ready access to online learning, there is a temptation to perhaps curtail the provision of seminary-type formation programmes and replace them with distance learning methodologies. In my view, nothing can replace the warmth of respectful and affirming hospitality, followed by the ability to discuss in a safe and closed community aspects of ministry which are challenging and problematic.

What aspects of your formation now seem most relevant to your current role?

The research questionnaire invited the respondents to indicate which aspects of their formation now seemed most relevant to their current role. The 1970s group were unreservedly enthusiastic and simply said "All of it." This was re-echoed by the 1980s group. One mentioned the relaxed and informal manner in which the weekly sessions had been carried out and that there was no homework! Another valued "anything of a catechetical nature – preaching for instance. Of course sermons must be doctrinally correct but if you've sat through as many doctrinally correct sermons as I have that were unutterably boring, you'd know that there has to be more to it than that." Those ordained in the 1990s were enthusiastic about their formation in scripture, but one respondent found this to be the only relevant aspect of his formation. Another thought the Wonersh course was "theoretical and spiritual-based with little practical application." To counterbalance this, one respondent not only found it helpful in developing a personal relationship with Jesus, but felt that "on the academic side, the encouragement and support of lecturers, directors and tutors was of great help in enabling me to resume a course of study after many years away from an academic environment. For me the study of the scriptures during formation and the guidance we received to help us understand and appreciate the scriptures has given me a wonderful tool with which to develop my study and love of scripture."

Formation in scripture again featured highly in the responses of the 2000s cohort with one deacon expressing it as "Scripture, scripture and scripture. Theology was good. But the other subjects (history of the Church, practical aspects of the sacraments) were poor." Other positive aspects were the fellowship of the other candidates, the experience of attending seminary and the discipline of the Divine Office, which for one respondent "shaped my being more than academic study, although essential." For another, the realisation that "there are almost as many views of faith as there are people was a new and valuable insight" and he felt that "everyone's faith journey is equally valid and has to be respected. I believe that this breadth of exposure and the mingling with other candidates from other dioceses with differing emphases of ministry, has, I hope, given me a more catholic view (in the true sense) and enabled me to foresee a ministry which must encompass all."

What helped you to mature in your development as a candidate for ordination?

In addressing this question, the respondents from the 1970s nominated their parish work as key underpinning for their development as deacons, with one specifically mentioning the dissemination of learning from the Second Vatican Council and feeding back to his bishop how this was received by the lay faithful. The support of spiritual directors, priests, fellow students and the interest shown by parishioners featured in the feedback from the

1980s group. This was endorsed by both the 1990s and 2000s groups. Overall, one of the most significant contributions to the deacons' development was the support from their wives. Some also had experienced life-changing transformation which they could never have calculated for nor expected. One respondent recalled "I guess at the beginning, the formation programme made me realise how naive I was about my faith – and that when you scratched the surface I had very little understanding about why I believed what I believed. There was almost anger, and perhaps some shame that I had reached this stage in life without apparently giving much thought or attempt at understanding my faith. The sessions with the spiritual directors were crucial to me in coming to terms with my then relationship with God and developing a relationship with Christ. By the end of the formation I guess the true surprise was how much I had learned about myself."

For personal reflection or for discussion in small groups

1. From your experience of the deacon's ministry, how important is that they have a structured formation programme which includes formal qualifications?
2. Do you think the deacon in the workplace should be a visible sign of Roman Catholic ministry or should he stay "below the radar"?

Endnotes

[1] Nowell, R.. 1968. *The Ministry of Service.* London: Burns and Oates. p.96
[2] Pope Paul VI. 1967. *Sacrum Diaconatus Ordinem General Norms for Restoring the Permanent Diaconate in the Latin Church* http://www.vatican.va/holy_father/paul_vi/motu_proprio/documents/hf_p-vi_motu-proprio_19670618_sacrum-diaconatus_en.html accessed 21/04/2013 – Libreria Editrice Vaticana (© Libreria Editrice Vaticana, 2013).
[3] Kasper, W. 2003. *Leadership in the Church.* New York: Crossroad. p.39.
[4] Fry, T. (ed) 1982. *The Rule of St Benedict in English.* Collegeville, Minnesota: The Liturgical Press. p.54.

5 | The Permanent Diaconate in the Context of the Threefold Ministry

The restoration of the permanent diaconate within the threefold ministry of bishop, priest and deacon was of course not the only ecclesiastical development of the Second Vatican Council. The role of the bishop was reappraised and expressed as "the fullness of order" with the priest and the deacon participating in the bishop's sacred threefold ministry to "teach, sanctify and lead". Although the bishop was "ordained" to the episcopate, the terms "installation" and "consecration" tended to be the norm. Clearly he was to be understood, not as an "office holder" of the diocese but ordained as its sacred minister. The minor orders were also re-examined and subsequently reconfigured to more readily address the needs of the contemporary Church. Replacing the sevenfold *Cursus Honorum* (linear route into Holy Orders consisting of porter, lector, acolyte, exorcist, subdeacon, deacon, priest) the orders of lector and acolyte were reconstituted as lay ministries for men, and the order of subdeacon was subsumed into the diaconate, which became the lowest level of sacred ministry.[1] (The gateway to Holy Orders was originally marked by the shearing of the candidate's hair in "first tonsure".)

As has already been noted, the deacon is ordained only by the bishop by the laying-on of hands, and not by the priests, thereby signifying the special relationship that exists between the deacon and his bishop. This theological body language may appear to be somewhat at variance with the lived reality of the deacon's ministry which is undertaken in very close collaboration with the parish priest. In this chapter, the actual experience of the deacon respondents in the Southwark Province study will be explored in the context of the complementarity of the ministries of the deacon, priest and bishop.

The responses of the entire research group were summarised without segregation into the decades in which they had been ordained. The deacons identified several "models" of relationship with the priest and bishops:
- The deacon as "filler of gaps"
- The deacon as "first responder" or as "safety net"
- The deacon as "bridge or "mediator"
- The deacon as "parson"
- The deacon as "the bishop's man"
- The deacon as "icon of the Holy Spirit"

The deacon as "filler of gaps"

Respondents referred to ministries undertaken because the priest was "too busy". These ministries included sacramental and pastoral provision – baptism, marriage preparation, burials and chaplaincy. Two respondents used the term "covering gaps" and another referred to "relieving priest of some faculties i.e. baptisms." One respondent spoke of "sharing and assisting with the liturgy, in preaching, in conducting those baptisms, weddings and funerals that do not appeal so much to the priest." Three immediate questions arise from this interpretation of the diaconate as a "filler ministry". Firstly, is the restored diaconate not perceived to be a theologically valid ministry in its own right within the threefold priesthood? Secondly, if there were more priests, would the deacon's role be seen as superfluous? The third question could perhaps be directed at priests themselves, "Why is a priest perceived to be too busy to officiate at Baptisms, marriages and funerals?" McKnight alludes to the deployment of deacons to meet sacramental and liturgical needs because of the dwindling number of priests. He feels that this comes at a cost to the diaconate itself as it "prevents the diaconate from developing its own unique identity and purpose as a legitimate and beneficial order among the People of God."[2]

The deacon as "first responder" or "safety net"

One respondent identified his role as "the first contact" for the parishioners and a helper to his elderly priest who serves two parish communities. The latter situation was also the experience of Respondent 362 who had increasingly become a safety net for a very frail and elderly parish priest. This support has been acknowledged by the bishop as a valued contribution to the pastoral care of the priests under his charge. It also means that the support of the deacon enables the priest to continue to live out his vocation in the parish. Whether it enables the deacon to live out his vocation in the parish may be the subject of conjecture.

The deacon as a "bridge" or mediator

Several respondents alluded to their ministry as a "bridge" between the priest and the people – "I find that some approach me regarding family problems with the children as they feel I can be a little more understanding" (Respondent 500). This view was endorsed by Respondent 338 as follows: "That one has a normal life: family, job, mortgage, money worries gives credibility. One is taken into confidences that are not shared with the priest." Respondent 393 expressed his role as follows, "I am out there among the people living and working with them. Because I have grown up in my parish I am (name) first – that is who they talk to, relate to, and I hope, trust, I am Deacon (name) second – the bridge between the people and the priest and bishop – if they need a bridge."

American theologian William McKnight cautions against an interpretation of the diaconate as an intermediate order (*medius ordo*) in so far as it might be seen as a linear progression through the hierarchy. Instead, he favours Pope Paul VI's interpretation of the diaconate as a "structure to express the needs and desires of the Christian faithful, to animate the membership of the Church to fulfil her obligation of charity and to serve as a symbol of Christ the servant to all."[3] McPartlan similarly is concerned about the bridge metaphor applied to the diaconate, since it might imply a gap between the institutional Church and the faithful which needs to be overcome. It is tempting to perceive the deacon as the bridge between the priest and the laity, since the deacon inhabits the secular world of work and family, whilst the priest is regarded as the holy man "set apart". In understanding the full significance of the bridge metaphor, it is useful to remember that this terminology had its roots in pre-Christianity. The word for "bridge-builder" is derived from the Latin *pons (*bridge*)* and bridge-builder (*pontifex* – a contraction of *pontis-factor* or "maker of the bridge." This term was used for the high priests of ancient Roman pagan religion and later was adopted by the Christian Church as a title for its bishops. The Pope is still referred to as the "Supreme Pontiff" although this term is not commonly used today.

The deacon as "parson"

Although borrowed from Anglicanism, the traditional view of the "parson of this place" can perhaps be recast for the role of the contemporary deacon who is resident in his parish whilst the priest may reside elsewhere and minister to more than one parish community. Respondent 490 referred to his initial role in the parish as being focused on youth and family ministries as the priest was older and of "longstanding in the parish. With a change (of priest), I am now a source of memory and continuity as a stable minister in this place." The most advanced model of "parson" deacon demonstrated by the data is one where the deacon "runs a parish with two churches. There is no resident parish priest – canon law requires a parish priest and he is the parish priest of an adjoining parish and we 'buy' priests in to preside at Mass, confer the Sacrament of Reconciliation and Anointing of the Sick as required. Everything else is delegated to me. That includes all administrative and pastoral care of the parishioners, baptisms, marriages, funerals etc save where I am unavailable."

The deacon as the "Bishop's man"

This role has its historical roots in the age of the Apostolic Fathers with 100-500 C.E. frequently cited as the "golden age" of the diaconate.[4] As assistants to the bishops, deacons had a major role in both administrative duties and liturgical functions and often succeeded the bishop in office.[5] Respondent 415 considered himself to be "one of the ears and eyes of the bishop," whilst Respondent

338 thought part of his role was to perhaps explain the bishop's thinking. Respondent 477 felt that, in contrast to other neighbouring parishes which were served by religious orders, he, in collaboration with the parish priest, was "very naturally the 'bishop's man'". Whilst one deacon, who is professionally employed by his diocese saw his role as assisting the bishop in his governance duties, the majority did not directly state how they perceived diaconal ministry in relation to the episcopate. Ditewig outlines the unique sacramental relationship which exists between the bishop and the deacon. Liturgically expressed at ordination when only the bishop lays hands on the ordinand, the deacon is "ordered" to a participation in the bishop's own ministry – *diakonia* of word, sacrament and charity in the Church. Ditewig notes that on certain occasions, some bishops continue to wear the deacon's dalmatic under their chasuble as a sign of their own diaconal responsibilities. He concludes "One often rightly hears of the special sacramental and sacerdotal relationship that bonds the bishop with his body of priests. One should also hear of an analogous sacramental and diaconal relationship that bonds the bishop – the chief deacon of the diocese – with his body of deacons."[6]

A corrective to any tendency to see the threefold ministry as a strictly differentiated division of labour comes in Pope Benedict's XVI's account of how Pope Paul VI was very moved by the ritual enthroning of the Book of the Gospels at the beginning of each working day of the Second Vatican Council. He asked if he might perhaps have the privilege of doing so, only to be told that he could not as it was the deacon's job! He noted in his diary "…but I am also a deacon, I continue to be a deacon and I would like to exercise the ministry of the diaconate placing the word of God on its throne."[7]

The deacon as icon of the Holy Spirit

Although only one respondent alluded to the deacon as "icon of the Holy Spirit" in the context of this particular question, it is a theme which occurs elsewhere in the research findings. Respondent 482 explains this diaconal model as follows: "It is a different ministry – but it complements what they do. We are a ministry of service to the Body of Christ in the power of the Holy Spirit – they (priests and bishops) have the power to make decisions. Although we can influence pastoral decisions, ultimately we have to go along with the hierarchy and do what the bishop and the priest want. It is like being a servant in some ways – a theologian said that the bishop is the icon of God the Father, the priest the icon of Jesus and the deacon the icon of the Holy Spirit. I could say or write a lot more on this!"

Although this respondent has not elaborated further, he is perhaps hinting at the developing understanding of the theology of the diaconate as expressed by Ditewig as follows:

> Theologies of diaconate, as indeed *all* theologies of *ministry* – must begin with a full appreciation of the power, risk and mystery of sacramental initiation into the Trinity. This provides a common sacramental identity while establishing the possibilities for creative, dynamic, Spirit-filled and transformative mission.

Ditewig cites Corbon's[8] identification of two *kenoses*, the *kenosis* of the Spirit and the *kenosis* of love. (The word *kenosis* in Greek means "self-emptying" and is frequently applied to Jesus in the pouring out of his entire self in accordance with his Father's will.)

> Having become the Church, we must live the Church's life as *kenosis* of the Spirit. The gift to us of God's ever faithful love must be answered by an authentic life of charity which the Holy Spirit pours into our hearts. We too must give of ourselves in that same *kenosis* of love.[9]

How do you think the parish priest perceives your role?

Because of the significance of this question, the responses are shown in full rather than being summarised. They have, however, been grouped to reflect themes which have emerged from the data.

Deacon as colleague or friend
A useful assistant who is also a colleague. He also never forgets my family commitments and duties.
Appreciation of short notice stand-in for activity when he is called away.
As a member of the clergy team working in the vineyard of the Lord.

As a specific ministry within his parish
…the *de iure* parish priest sees my role as doing everything save what I cannot do. (Note: *de iure* refers to the status of the priest in Church law.)
As an assistant and the point of contact when he is absent from the parish.
Re new priest "I did emphasise to him that I was willing to do what he wishes….even if that meant nothing as I did not want discord between us. I have always ensured that there is no conflict so we act as a team with me doing anything that he either thinks I am better at or has no time to do himself."
My current parish priest is totally supportive of the permanent diaconate. My relationship with him although positive, unsurprisingly, is very different than that I enjoyed with his predecessor; but then we live in different times with different challenges, particularly for him. I would put this down perhaps to a degree of similarity of personality. I am unsure, however, to what extent he would concur with that thought!
My current PP sees me as a co-worker in the vineyard. We meet weekly and discuss all aspects of the parish, including what he thinks I should do. As he is the Catholic chaplain at the local hospital, we cooperate in making sure that pastoral care continues when they transfer to either hospice, nursing or residential homes in the area.
Clerical, part of joint responsibility for parish, catechesis, key liturgical/sacramental role.
Parish priest was one who agreed to put me forward and we seem to work well together. He does not view me as an assistant "priest" but as a deacon and we sit down from the beginning and agree what I shall do most effectively to help parish.
He says a great friend who works together.

Deacon as "curate"
I am respected almost as if I were the curate.
Like a curate!
…my first parish priest thought of me as a curate and treated me as one, giving no consideration to my having any personal or family commitments.
They all perceive it slightly differently. With my current PP we are still new to each other. My previous had me, in some respects, as the curate he never had. I think with them all I am the sheep dog to their shepherd role.
My new parish priest sometimes regards me as an equal – at other times as a curate.

Collaborative ministry
My subsequent parish priests were considerate in seeking to match their needs and my availability, generally being thankful for what I can do and accepting limitations on my availability. Much more like a symbiotic relationship.
Currently, he is encouraging about the work that I do and understands when I have to concentrate on other things such as family or my work for Fathers Prayers.
I think both see the role as some of the parish, supporting him and the other lay ministers and parish as a whole.
Having served under three parish priests, all have different opinions of the diaconate varying from cool to enthusiastic.
He allows me to work to my strengths.
It differs between priests. Most understand the need for me to take part in the word, sacrament and charity.

He has been very supportive and has constantly emphasised the sacramental nature of diaconate. I think- well I know- that he has appreciated my support and my homilies.
My PP is good and has an above average insight into diaconate- he is exceptional in this regard.
He's only been here a week so we have yet to find out. However his predecessors have been very good to me but, as I say, it does help to remember that I am not a priest and have to remember to step back on occasions and let him be what he is.
Helper and support, both to fill gaps and take some of the pressure off him. As a sounding board for new ideas.
My present parish priest involves me in all aspects of parish life including sacramental preparation, preaching and hospital chaplaincy.
As a member of the parish team.
Of value and comfort.
He offers me as much space and opportunity as I want, whilst not overloading me with burdensome demand, or expectation. Within the parish, I think he sees me as someone who can assist him pastorally and liturgically – although in a limited way – and who can bring a different perspective than his own.
Positively. I look after some baptisms and fit in wherever family allows.
Very much as part of the parish team (there is also a priest curate) and always very supportive of any ideas I might have re pastoral ministry.
With (word indecipherable) support and has a full understanding of the deacon's ministry.

Ambivalence expressed
He appreciates my work but he does not see me as a colleague: rather as someone to fall back on when he is desperate.
God only know! Ask him.
He likes the idea but only occasionally consults, encourages or makes demands.
He sees me as a willing and reliable helper in the background, but not as a close colleague or friend.
I am still working on that.
I try to do the things that I can, and do them the best I can.
With gratefulness I think!

Models of leadership issues
I find this difficult to gauge as it seems to vary. Sometimes he is inclusive and I genuinely feel like we are brother clergy sharing a ministry, but then he reverts to a "traditional" priest where all power and authority are vested in him and he makes decisions without regard to how that may impact on my ministry. I think that it's acceptance and toleration, and support on a day to day basis, provided that it doesn't impinge on the priest's ministry. I know that your question is specifically aimed at my local situation, but generally I think that many priests don't know what to do with deacons.
I have had three parish priests to date. The first two I worked as part of their team in carrying out their vision for the parish. My present role is much similar but as my priest is much set in his ways, I have to anticipate more.
I have worked for (number) here in (place). Yes I have had my ups and downs with most of them – all of them. I have won many battles, but I have made firm friends of them all.

| The Permanent Diaconate in the Context of the Threefold Ministry

I have worked with several. Mostly, it was appreciated. But it is a recognised fact among deacons that some priests do not want them or see the point of them!
I think he perceives my role as supporting him in his desires rather than seeing it in a collaborative sense. Seminaries need to update their methods of teaching so that collaborative ministry is better understood.
This is a difficult question as I have (number) parish priests since being ordained and each have their own views. Some have involved me in taking on a very active role and making me an active member of the core team of the parish. Others have kept me on the fringe by not being very communicative of what is happening in the parish. Communication is virtually nil. I just continue to do what I have done over the years – both in administrative and charity roles, My involvement in the "breaking of the word" varies from good to minimal (What message does this convey?)

Duties in addition to the deacon's threefold ministry
Since I retired I no longer serve on the sanctuary on Sundays. I am responsible for all the parish registers and deal with requests for baptismal and marriage certificates, Letters of Freedom etc. I am an Authorised Person for Marriages and complete the quarterly returns for the Registrar. I act as a consultant on matters concerning entries to the registers.

11 comments (20.75%) classified "Deacon as Colleague" are those which indicate a strong interpersonal relationship between the deacon and his parish priest. When experienced positively, the priest values his deacon as a brother-minister in Holy Orders and as a friend. Negatively, the relationship has been expressed by three respondents as "like a curate" although two respondents regard the curate status as a compliment. Although the main focus of this research project was the ministry of the deacon, there is perhaps some justification for advocating reflection on the ongoing support provided to newly ordained priests when they are assigned to their parishes. In some instances, there would appear to be a prevailing culture of, at best, "tough love" and at worst, bullying. These behaviours may have been inculcated by priests as a result of their own earlier experiences in parish. However, this is an endeavour outside the scope of this present work.

Under the title "Collaborative Ministry" are 18 comments (33.9%) which reflect an integrated parish structure where diaconal contributions are valuable in the context of the whole. Together with the comments made by those deacons who are regarded as trusted colleagues and friends, the overall experience of 41 respondents has been positive (77.36%). These findings accord with

Geary's results from the 2007 Ushaw study in which he invited deacons to identify which of the following terms best described their relationship with the parish priest. It was found that 39.29% of Southwark Province deacons regarded the parish priest as a "colleague", 17.86% regarded him as a "friend", with a further 21.4% classifying the relationship as that with a "line-manager", or "team leader". 5.36% regarded the parish priest as a "father figure" and 3.57% were simply designated "other" without further elaboration. When asked to select from a list of options to describe the relationship with the parish priest, 5.4% selected "difficult", 10.7% chose "distant", 8.9% selected "neutral", whilst 30.4% selected "co-operative" and 44.6% selected "excellent". In summary, both studies indicate a positive relationship with the parish priest for over three-quarters of the deacons taking part in the research projects (77.36% in current study and 75% in 2007 Ushaw study).

Within this present cohort, however, are some who have also experienced unsatisfactory interrelationships with their previous parish priests. 7 comments (13.21%) garnered under the title "Ambivalence Expressed" speak of a somewhat uncertain relationship with the parish priest – tolerance rather than warmth, timidity rather than confidence. 6 comments (11.32%) classified under "Models of Leadership" highlight ministry undertaken against a problematic backdrop of uncertainty and sometimes negativity. Respondents are unsure if their role is really understood and perceive their value to the parish priest in terms of a "filler ministry" i.e. to undertake those duties which the parish priest is too busy to perform.

Two possible explanations for this situation will be briefly explored at this stage. Firstly, it is possible that, due to the relatively undeveloped state of the contemporary diaconate, it is simply perceived as "less than priesthood" and "little more than laity". Secondly, the unease in the relationships between priests and deacons may relate to a hierarchical interpretation of parish leadership in which the priest directs and controls all facets of ministry and parish life.

Complementarity of deacon, priest and bishop

In considering the complementarity of the three ministries which comprise sacred order, the deacon respondents have articulated clearly the impact on their pastoral practice of the relationships which they have forged within their communities. What is less clearly expressed is the link with the episcopate. Although the sacramental link is well understood, it appears that there are few opportunities for the deacons to realize their role as social intermediaries who represent the needs of the people. This is a vital role for the deacon as a minister of service, as he is particularly well placed to advocate for those who are on the margins of the community.

In the 1983 *Code of Canon Law*, Can. 383 §1 speaks of the bishop's concern for:

> ...all the Christian faithful entrusted to his care, of whatever age, condition, or nationality they are, whether living in the territory or staying there temporarily; he is also to extend an apostolic spirit to those who are not able to make sufficient use of ordinary pastoral care because of the condition of their life and to those who no longer practice their religion.

Even more challenging is the need to provide for the:

> ...needs of the faithful of a different rite in his diocese, ...(providing) for their spiritual needs either through priests or parishes of the same rite or through an episcopal vicar.

He is also to act:

> ...with humanity and charity toward the brothers and sisters who are not in full communion with the Catholic Church and is to foster ecumenism as it is understood by the Church.

Finally,

> ...he is to consider the non-baptized as committed to him in the Lord, so that there shines on them the

charity of Christ whose witness a bishop must be before all people.[10]

So where does the deacon feature in this awesome line-up? He is the only minister in Roman Catholic Holy Orders who may have a secular job, the only one permitted to undertake a role in civic life and the only one who can witness to the call of Christ in the way he orders his family life and marriage. He is not a man set apart in the way that priests and bishops are set apart. That is his strength and his greatest challenge. He is a form of ecclesiastical amphibian who inhabits two environments. It could be argued that far from being "the easy way", to use Spellman's notorious words, the permanent diaconate is a more difficult vocation to follow, since it calls for a selfless giving without the status usually accorded to priest and bishop. As mentioned in the Introduction, one of the respondents summed up the complementarity of his ministry with that of priest and bishop as: "Primarily by being married, by living in the real world where the mortgage has to be paid, the gutters cleared, the kids' vomit mopped up, the groceries bought. By standing in the dole queue. By having sex. By suffering. Very few priests and bishops have done all that. So the people can talk to you about it, in the belief that you will understand."

How were you received as a new deacon in your parish by the parish priest, lay ministers and the congregation?

In further exploring the dynamic of the threefold ministry of the deacon within the threefold ministry of sacred order, the deacons were asked to reflect on how they had been received in their parish by the parish priest, lay ministers and the congregation at large. In answering the question in relation to the parish priest, there was 1 "nil response" to this question. 40 (75.5%) of the respondents indicated that they had been warmly welcomed by their parish priests, some of whom had been instrumental in discerning the deacons' vocations, and, in one instance, had also been the tutor/supervisor during the formation period. Others, however, had a more guarded relationship with their parish priest. Respondent 457's experience was "initially with caution but as he (the parish priest) grew in confidence and trust, he engaged me more fully in sharing in the ministry" whilst Respondent 458's account highlighted a fundamental distrust felt by the priest in relation to his deacon – "he was never able to adjust to having me around. On the altar, he regarded me (and said he would regard any other cleric) as a pair of eyes watching him and checking up on him so he was never at ease. He treated me as if I were his curate rather than as a deacon and much of his behaviour probably reflected how he had been poorly treated as a curate in years past." The experience of Respondent 371 was similar, insofar as his parish priest thought that the deacon had been ordained so that he could "spy on him for the bishop" and then, perhaps in some way replace the priest. "It took a good couple of years for a working and trusting relationship to develop." Respondent 445's experience was even more problematic in that he perceived his parish priest to have been jealous of his professional qualifications and family life and manifested this in making unreasonable demands, which the deacon found tantamount to bullying. Respondent 316 had not been allowed to hold a key to either the church or the presbytery, and his parish priest publicly expressed the view that deacons were only needed to "look after the place when the parish priest is away". The final observation on this question relates to the payment of "stole" fees. (Stole fees are donations given to the minister who conducts baptisms, officiates at weddings and conducts funerals.) Respondent 415 found that his parish priest, whilst welcoming diaconal involvement in ministry to those in residential care, was reluctant to have his deacon take part in any ministry which earned a stole fee. This deacon conducted his first funeral after five years in ministry.

 The experiences of the deacons in this research would indicate that there is still some misunderstanding as to their role and function. The tensions identified in relation to the presbyterate (ministry of the priest) may well relate to what Barnett describes as the "omniverious priesthood". He takes the view that the single model of ministry i.e. ordained priesthood is "like a persistent virus that infects our thinking and acting in subtle but insidious ways."[11] For example, the seminary model of training, the deployment of deacons to deputise for the priest while he is absent and the outward symbols of presbyteral priesthood i.e. Roman collars, black suits and the title "reverend" perpetuate a limited and rather myopic view of *diakonia*. If this view is held by the priest, there may be tension, misunderstanding and the type of mistrust which has been evident in the current data.

From a researcher's perspective. it is interesting to observe the gradual clericalisation of student deacons and later the clerical persona which is inculcated as they are assimilated into their role. The wearing of clerical garb has been noted and the tendency for some deacons to be even more observant in the wearing of black suits and Roman collars than their priest colleagues.

How were you received as a new deacon in your parish by the lay ministers?

There were 4 "nil responses" and 45 (85%) who responded positively to this question. For the earliest cohort of the 1970s, there had been no lay ministries at the time of their ordination. Nonetheless, they managed to establish collaborative models of ministry when the new ministerial functions were developed. Respondent 454 noted that one lay minister felt threatened that her role would be undermined, whilst Respondent 458 thought that he was initially perceived as "a threat by one or two parishioners who felt he might undermine "their longstanding relationship (i.e. influence over!) the parish priest." Respondent 393 was keen to ensure that "the diaconate did not become a barrier between me and anyone else" – specifically, he would never seek to administer the chalice at Communion if the designated lay minister was present. Many of the respondents had emerged from the communities in which they had lived for most of their lives and had borne witness to their faith both sacramentally and pastorally in the presence of those to whom they now ministered. This reassured the lay ministers that they were not being superseded or their ministry devalued.

How were you received as a new deacon in your parish by the congregation?

There were 4 "nil responses" to this question and 42 (79%) indicating a very high level of support and joyful welcome by their congregations. However, due to lack of understanding of the role of deacon, some lay people were puzzled or perturbed. Respondent 495 expressed it as follows "Suddenly seeing somebody else touching the Host and distributing the Eucharist, touching the sacred vessels and opening and shutting the tabernacle door was a great shock. However, as time went on, attitudes began to change for the better. I suppose I could be described as a pioneer, paving the way for lay ministers of communion and lay readers being accepted." Respondent 478 noted hostility in a few members of his congregation to a married man being vested and being in the sanctuary during Mass. Respondent 500, although well received by the congregation, was aware of "line switching in the queues away from me when coming up to receive the Body of Christ." Happily, this did not last too long. In the case of Respondent 415, however, "lane switching" prevailed for much longer and it took ten years before he was fully accepted.

In summary, it would appear that the deacons were generally well received by their communities and any reservations related to the acceptance of an emerging ministry and a poorly articulated theology of the diaconate as a permanent state in Holy Orders.

How were you helped to settle into your role?

There were 4 "nil responses" to this question. 25 respondents (47.2%) specifically identified the support of their parish priest as the cornerstone of their new ministry. Others used general terms like "encouragement" "everyone was helpful in their constructive criticism", "by being given space and opportunity", "by kindness and support of the whole parish" – these of course may have included the parish priest but were not specifically stated as such. Three respondents mentioned the affirmation of deanery priests and curates and two identified peer support from other deacons. The support of spouses and family members was highlighted by six respondents. Respondent 424 recalled that "There was not much help. Sort of 'find your own feet'" whilst Respondent 316 found the process "just difficult all round. The lack of understanding by my PP and his unwillingness to discuss my role was a severe handicap in developing my ministry. I think that in some way he felt threatened by my ordination and I got the impression that he was jealous of the fact that I had academic qualifications from my previous life while he had none." For Respondent 362, this aspect of his new role was "most disappointing due to the priest's view that it was a private affair until nearing ordination. Then I had no visible support from him or the parish. There was a great opportunity missed for the parish to share in supporting the formation period, through prayer or sharing properly in the stages of candidacy (Reader and Acolyte). I had contemplated giving up part way through as I had begun to view this as a ministry which nobody wanted. Not surprisingly, there really was no help in the parish in settling into the role." It was only through the support of his supervisor (a religious sister) during the first year of his ministry that this deacon began to make sense of the vocation to which he believed he had been called.

In what respects (if any) is the permanent diaconate how you expected it to be?

9 respondents declined to answer this question whilst 22 (41.5%) found that the ministry was as they expected it. They variously described this as "all aspects of it. It was a great joy", "generally as expected", "it is what I expected during my period of training, particularly the liturgical role", "no surprises", "During the long selection process (about six months as I recall) we were pretty well briefed." Others found that it exceeded their expectations: "I did not know what to expect but I am completely happy with my role, the way I/we are treated and regarded by the bishop and priest and by parishioners generally" (Respondent 397); "I think it's so much more, the blessing of such a vocation and the appreciation by the people unquestionable" (Respondent 491); "Much more fulfilling I certainly feel God has bestowed more graces upon me" (Respondent 417). This respondent linked his response to the earlier question about the discernment of his vocation, admitting frankly that until

midway through the second year of his formation he did not really know what a deacon did. Two deacons alluded to their ministry as one of presence to the community – "I am certainly not 'assistant PP' but I am used where possible. Sometimes more of a 'ministry of presence"(Respondent 427) and "Throughout the period of formation the emphasis was not on what a deacon did, but what a deacon was – Christ present amongst his people. I feel that after some five or six years, that experience of the diaconate can, and has, become a reality for me" (Respondent 362).

In what respects (if any) is the permanent diaconate not what you expected it to be?

12 deacons (22.6%) chose not to respond to this question and one simply put "I cannot answer – sorry." 8 responses highlighted poor relationships with other clergy. Respondent 424 spoke of "feeling often of being only a second-class citizen of the hierarchy. I think deacons are taken advantage of. Priests get all the perks." Respondent 355 expressed his disappointment at how some priests perceive deacons – "somewhat dismissive" whilst Respondent 490 "did not expect even senior priests in the dioceses to be antagonistic towards my ministry. I did not see the politics before my ordination and wrongly assumed acceptance." In similar vein, Respondent 445 found that "a hefty percentage of priests struggle with the permanent deacons, wives etc. In fact the bishop actually said a permanent deacon is not a clergy member. I disagreed of course." Respondent 495 expressed surprise that many deacons "tend to adopt a purely cultic role and become too quickly identified with the clerical state – wishing to be called 'Reverend' to wear black suits and clerical collar… Deacons today attend deanery meetings wearing clerical collars which they remove to go home. How daft" (Respondent 495). Other issues identified were the lack of clarity around the deacon's role but this was seen in a positive light by two respondents who felt they could carve out their own role within the parish. One was not sure if this attitude made him "a maverick" (Respondent 399) whilst the other noted that "if the PP is obstructive, this is difficult, if not impossible" (Respondent 316). Some respondents had not expected the role to be so demanding. Respondent 478

found that individual parishioners made many demands upon his time and he had to learn to correct the balance between Church and home. Respondent 500 had not expected to "stand in for the parish priest when he does not want to attend ecumenical functions. I am happy to attend in my own right and when expected to by the Fraternal of the town parish. I had not expected to take the role in the inter-denominational meetings of the various churches in the town/borough. I had expected to be considered as clergy by the Roman Catholic denomination." This attitude is particularly interesting in the light of the Church's social teaching alluded to earlier and the various civic/secular roles in which deacons of the province are involved.

On a more positive note, some respondents felt that their diaconal role was what they expected and, in some instances, exceeded their expectations e.g. "Nerves are replaced by a sense of privilege" (Respondent 356), "I am not sure that I came with hugely specific expectations. I am doing what I expected to be doing and am being (by the grace of God) and becoming (ditto) what I expected to be and become" (Respondent 420).

The continued legacy of the *Cursus Honorum*

The situations described under "Leadership Issues" and in the "curate" comments may be symptomatic of an unhelpful "*cursus honorum*" attitude to the permanent diaconate. (This relates to the graduated ministries of the medieval period consisting of porter, lector acolyte etc eventually leading to deacon, priest and bishop). Barnett outlines the problem of giving permanent deacons a title which their priest colleagues are assigned only temporarily en route to higher orders. He takes the view that transitional deacons are:

> ...not called to the diaconate, are not trained for the diaconate and do not serve diaconal ministries, except in the broader sense. They are in fact called to be priests, trained to be priests, and usually serve essentially priestly ministries after being ordained deacons. Such terms (i.e. permanent and transitional) compromise the integrity of the diaconate and degrade the office. The term 'deacon' should stand alone without any modifying term, when

the reference is to a real deacon, one called to that office, trained for that office and ordained to serve in that office as a permanent vocation.[12]

Barnett concludes that "if any adjective is used, it should be 'transitional' and used to designate the transitional diaconate only." He believes that this "will serve to recover the integrity of the office as the separate and equal order it was in the early church".[13] Some would be even more radical than Barnett, suggesting the abolition of the term "transitional diaconate" entirely or, indeed, the order itself, in much the same way as the minor orders of exorcist, porter and tonsure were suppressed because they were no longer considered appropriate or valid ways of expressing vocation. Such a radical step may serve to designate the diaconate as a valid, separate and equal order and "facilitate a truer discernment of what one's fundamental vocation might be."[14] Such a development might lend ecclesiastical credibility to a ministry, the pastoral credentials of which are largely seen by lay people as fully vindicated, but may still meet with skepticism from the presbyterate i.e. the priests.

It is possible that some parish priests feel less affirmed in their own presbyteral role, now no longer seen as the "fullness of priesthood". The discomfiture expressed in earlier responses about the deacon being sent to "spy" upon the priest and being "the bishop's man" may contribute to such an atmosphere of distrust.

Giftedness

The deacons were then invited to consider which aspects of the diaconal role most fitted their personalities and giftedness. There was 1 "nil response" to this question. 8 respondents simply answered "Charity" to this question without further elaboration, whilst others configured it with the other ministries of the deacon e.g. "visiting the sick, housebound, those in hospital, the dying and their families, also in spiritual direction in my role as chaplain (to a public service)" (Respondent 458), "my experience as a prison chaplain, preparing couples for marriage, work on marriage annulments all point to the gift of charity" (Respondent 415). Respondent 441 expressed it as "charity and word. Conveying the meaning of the Eucharist", thereby setting his charitable role in the context of the sacrificial giving of Christ in the Eucharist. Respondent 457 devoted 40+ hours per week to works of charity and added that "I find preaching demanding, but a number of parishioners say they find my reflections on the Sunday Scriptures helpful." This respondent, although not entirely comfortable with preaching, was clearly able to inspire his community with the pastoral insights he brought to his homiletics. For Respondent 386, the role of charity included caring, counselling and visiting the sick, whilst Respondent 500 linked the ministry of charity to the sacramental preparation of parishioners for baptism and marriage. Respondent 395 said simply "My greatest gift is the ability to sit quietly with people. I think that is charity, but it is also a sign and silent proclamation." Respondent 362 noted that having completed a *Gallup Strengthfinders Analysis*, he had identified his key characteristics as "developer, relator, connectedness, harmony and includer." These qualities manifested themselves in looking for the best in people around him and recognizing the "spiritual force at work in bringing harmony to this group of people and extending this to all with whom I come in contact." His insights led him to conclude: "My diaconal role enables me to come into contact and work with a whole range of people across the parish and in the wider pastoral community – and, by the grace of God, can help them to become the people that God wants them to be. Through the ministry of the word, I pray that I can communicate God's love for his people and the destiny to which they could aspire." Respondent 420 expressed this as follows: "Academically, I am not suited to the former (ministry of the word), and professionally to the latter (ministry of charity) whereas in terms of personal taste, the middle one (sacrament) appeals. I feel very strongly that the grace of the Sacrament of Order works to ensure an integrity and that one does not get one *munus (*ministerial role*)* to the detriment of the other *munera (*ministerial roles*)*; if grace builds on nature, then the deacon needs to find a fit for all three, and to do otherwise is harmful." 8 respondents felt that all three areas of ministerial service were of equal importance and tried to honour these appropriately. Respondent 316 with humble candour admitted "I find this most difficult to answer. I am still not sure as to why God wanted me to be a deacon, but I suppose he sees something in me which I cannot. However, my training in industry in giving presentations and in how to make the most of other people's talents has been very useful, as have my coordinating and administrative skills."

The responses to this question indicate that the deacons do not perceive their ministry as three separate functions, but rather as a complex interrelationship whereby the experience and insights from each ministry enriches and complements the others. Their understanding reflects the views of Ditewig who, in tracing the "first stirrings of a renewed diaconate" in Germany in the nineteenth and twentieth centuries cautions against seeing the ministry as a movement for enhanced works of charity but rather as part of an overall movement of renewal and providing a context for a relationship between the Church and the modern world."[15]

For personal reflection or for discussion in small groups

1. Thinking of your own experience of the ministry of deacons, what preparations would you suggest for a parish about to have its first deacon?
2. If you were invited to draw up a "personal profile" of a deacon, which qualities would you list and why?

Endnotes

[1] Pope Paul VI. 1973. Apostolic Letter *Ministeria Quaedam* http://www.ewtn.com/library/papaldoc/p6minors.htm accessed 04/05/2012

[2] McKnight, W.S. 2006. "The Deacon as a *Medius Ordo*: Service in Promotion of Lay Participation" in Keating, J. (ed) 2006. *The Deacon Reader.* New York: Paulist Press.p.79.

[3] Ibid. p.83.

[4] Ditewig. W.T. 2007 *The Emerging Diaconate.* New York: Paulist Press. pp.62-65.

[5] Barnett J.M. 1995. *The Diaconate – a Full and Equal Order.* Harrisburg: Trinity Press p.43.

[6] Ditewig. W.T. 2007 *The Emerging Diaconate.* New York: Paulist Press.pp.135-136.

[7] McConvery, B.2010. "The Deacon and the Ministry of the Word" in Dullea, E (ed). *2010 Deacons – Ministers of Christ and of God's Mysteries.* Dublin: Veritas. p.55.

[8] Corbon, J. 1988. *The Wellspring of Worship.* New York: Paulist. pp.106-7 cited in Ditewig, W.T. 2007 *The Emerging Diaconate.* New York: Paulist Press p.130.

[9] Ditewig, W.T. 2007. *The Emerging Diaconate.* New York: Paulist Press pp.128-130.

[10] Code of Canon Law. 1983. http://www.vatican.va/archive/ENG1104/__P1E.HTM accessed 21/4/2013 – Libreria Editrice Vaticana (© Libreria Editrice Vaticana, 2013).

[11] Barnett, J.M. 1995. The *Diaconate - A Full and Equal Order.* Harrisburg: Trinity Press. p.154.

[12] Ibid p.148.

[13] Ibid p.148.

[14] One of the "critical friends" of the project, an academic theologian involved in seminary formation (September 2008).

[15] Ditewig, W.T. 2007. *The Emerging Diaconate.* New York: Paulist Press. p.146.

6 | CAN A DEACON BE A LEADER?

This is a question which many parishioners and perhaps some parish priests ponder regarding the permanent diaconate. It is a question which many deacons probably ask themselves. The Southwark Province research questionnaire invited deacons to describe their style of leadership and gave some examples of possible responses e.g. "like to lead from the front", "prefer to work in the background", "like to work within a group", "prefer to work alone on projects", "like to be involved in every aspect of the project", "prefer to work with the 'big picture'", "like to direct", "good at delegating" etc.

Hovering in the background is, of course, the question of the nature of *diakonia* and how this is manifested in the roles which deacons undertake. At its simplest, the question is: "Can you be a servant and a leader at one and the same time?" to which the simplest response is: "Jesus was." Jesus demonstrated all the qualities of the servant leader. He had authority, which he acknowledged was from his Heavenly Father. The gospel accounts of the revelation of Christ as the Messiah leave no doubt that Jesus is a figure of authority. Mark's gospel testifies to the endorsement of the Father when Jesus emerges from his baptism in the Jordan: "You are my Son, the Beloved; my favour rests on you" (Mark 1:11.) In Luke 4:32, Jesus impresses the listeners in Capernaum because "he spoke with authority". However, he is also the leader who cautions his followers against behaving like the pagan kings "who lord it over" their people. He says: "This must not happen with you. No, the greatest among you must behave as if he were the youngest, the leader as if he were the one who serves" (Luke 22:24-27). John's gospel of course recounts the mandate of Jesus to wash one another's feet in imitation of the Lord (John 13:1-15). Taking Jesus as **the** exemplary deacon, the contemporary deacon can confidently and humbly minister as both servant and leader.

So what of the Southwark Province deacons? 14 deacons (26%) identified "leading from the front" as their main style of leadership. Some saw this as a vehicle for empowering others and they deployed management styles which they normally used in their professional lives to motivate and encourage people within their parishes. As one expressed it: "I am a 'big picture' rather than a details leader who likes to leave people to get on with their own responsibilities, with a minimum of interference from me. I am not averse to the 'up-front' role and see accountable decisiveness as essential. I am happy working in teams but aware that collaboration is often used as a cover for avoiding responsibility for decision-making, for which it is no substitute."

12 respondents (23%) described a "coaching" style of leadership as more in keeping with their personalities. One of these described it as follows: "My style of leadership is such that I look for people with skills that could be of benefit to the Church. I would ask them to take the lead in discussion with parishioners so that they could encourage people to assist them, utilising such a gift to develop the Church's ministry. I would prefer to work in the background, demonstrating that no one person has all the gifts needed to promote Church activity."

The third main style could be described as "collaborative", with 20 respondents (38%) identifying themselves within this category with comments like: "Fit in with what is required, being careful to respect what is already being done by others, act in such a way (in everything) that others can take over", and "I describe myself as the toolbox -available for all to use in whatever way for whatever reason. When completed, I am put back in the box."

One respondent preferred to work on projects where he was the sole contributor, whilst two others nominated themselves as able to both lead from the front and work in the background. The remaining deacon mentioned "servant leadership" by name as he liked the idea of "upside down hierarchies and where the leadership is shown in unexpected, symbolic examples of practical service". For completeness, there were four "Nil returns" to this question.

Having described their style of leadership in practical terms, the deacons were then invited to devise metaphors to describe their leadership style. Unlike the more prosaic description of their interactions, the metaphor provided a more creative, imaginative and aspirational way of describing their diaconal service. One of the respondents found it difficult to describe his style of leadership in this way and invited a number of people from within his community to offer their suggestions. Among the 11 responses were the followings:

> "The harness cords of a parachute – supportive, helpful, indeed necessary but I sometimes have the sense of us all getting rather tangled up."
>
> "A bear – sometimes growling and grumpy, sometimes misunderstood but always warm-hearted and cuddly!!!! Oh and very thoughtful."
>
> "A kind of sheep in a wolf's clothing."

Responses offered by the other deacons themselves were:

"St Stephen – one of the first deacons and the first Christian martyr. The only way they could shut him up was by stoning him."
"Yes, Minister!"
"Servus servorum Dei."
"I think 'one of the twelve' would suit me."
"I feel drawn to St Barnabas who was a companion to St Paul, without attaining Paul's fame or notoriety."
"I feel that people would – and do- come for advice. Yes, perhaps I could be – and sometimes am – a small Moses."
"A cross between Martha and maintenance engineer."
"Cor! That's interesting. Winston Churchill."
"I try to be a servant to the servants of God."
"Shepherd."
"One of the parish team."
"The image I like to keep in mind and apply to my ministry is that of Jesus washing the feet of the apostles during the Last Supper."
"Jonah, reluctantly pushed forward but who rose to the challenge!"
"First among equals, servant of the servants of God."
"Probably as 2IC." (Second in command).

"I once used Chelsea FC for my metaphor. Abramovitch is the owner (God), 'Big Phil' Scolari is the manager (the Bishop), but the coaching staff is where you'll find the deacons. Working alongside the players(that is, the congregation) – those with skills, the flair – with the aim of bring out the best in them. Definitely a 'coach'."
"I see myself as a bridge builder between people and priest, between the Church and the world."
"I am a leader, follower and one of the twelve. At the heart of the diaconate is charity/love – those two commandments of service – Love God above all things. Love your neighbour as yourself."
"Increasingly my style of leadership is more spiritual than didactic or liturgical. I try to set an example and approach by the way I live my faith life, as distinct from my Church /Religious life."
"Like St Stephen and the others of the seven in Acts, I'm there to assist the Church's pastors in serving the Church i.e. God's people. This means, like them, I end up doing a variety of things, but always under the authority of my bishop (perhaps even like Stephen, only to be martyred!)"
"The King who goes to a far country and commits talents to the stewards."
"To be a 'Good Shepherd' who knows his limitations."
"Washing feet."

It is interesting that the "*Servus Servorum Dei*" (Servant of the Servants of God) title has been used either in its Latin form or translated by three of the respondents. The term of course, attributed to Pope Gregory the Great around 545, whilst he was still a deacon, is thought to have come into general use by successive popes since the pontificate of Gregory VII (1073-85).[1] It could be argued that a term which betokens such abasement contrasts markedly with the monarchical and somewhat autocratic demeanour of the papal office. Whether this dichotomy applies equally to those in diaconal ministry can only be speculated upon. As for the sporting metaphor, based on Chelsea Football Club, it is probably encouraging for bishops that their tenure is more secure than Premier League football management.

"Fiduciary" leadership

In seeking to identify appropriate models of leadership which fittingly reflect diaconal self-giving, it might be appropriate to explore Max De Pree's theory of Servant-Leadership as a foil to the traditional hierarchical structure prevailing within the institutional Church, including the *cursus honorum*. In his work, De Pree explores the "fiduciary nature of leadership"[2], which, in a Church setting is rather akin to stewardship. This model has been highlighted by Ditewig as one which offers potential for pastoral application within the diaconate.

The term "fiduciary" is used in legal and other ethical contexts to describe a special relationship of trust which exists between, for example, a lawyer and client, a doctor and patient. It is built on good faith, good conscience and the concept of "holding in trust". Within the context of the Church, fiduciary leadership may be exercised by many in the community and not restricted to those in ecclesiastical office. It is a leadership style which promotes stewardship and the exercise of gifts and talents held by all members of the community and the holding in trust for future generations.

The second characteristic of this leadership style is that of learning and collaboration. De Pree explains that:

> By making it possible for people to grow and to work together, fiduciary leaders try to invest and enlarge the knowledge and talent that they hold in trust for individuals.[3]

Ditewig notes that "it is not a considerable stretch to see this path as necessary in a parish at all levels" and he notes that Church encyclicals and documents from Bishops' Conferences underscore adult faith formation as the responsibility of all and essential to parish life.

The third characteristic of this style of leadership is the balance struck between the related ideas of the individual and the concept of the community. This accountability, according to Ditewig is not restricted to the hierarchical chain of command but also to those who are served. It is a *communio* approach which is called into existence by God rather than by the force of the leader's will or an ecclesiastical *fiat*.

The fourth characteristic of fiduciary leadership is the building up of trust – this is the "coin of the realm" and the means through which collaboration, learning and *communio* are achieved. De Pree sees trust as "the basis of covenantal relationships which are far more productive than contractual ones."[4] Ditewig in considering this concept points to Kasper's insight which he applies to the role of the diaconate, but equally well it might be applied to presbyters: "The task is to bring a healing that sets people free and empowers them to trust and so to serve and love others in their turn."[5] This characteristic resonates with the sacrificial servant leadership of Christ which was explored earlier.

The final characteristic of the fiduciary leader is the leaving of a legacy. De Pree explains this in the context of *Gaudium et Spes* "The future is in the hands of those who can give tomorrow's generations reasons to live and hope" (GS31). De Pree's fiduciary leadership model offers an affirming and empowering template not only for the actualization of diaconal vocation but arguably, for the vocations of the priest/presbyter and the lay faithful too.

The Southwark Province deacons were invited to complete the following "Leadership" statements:

"I lead the following ministries…"

"Other things I would like to do but feel unable to…"

"I feel I am most a deacon when I …"

For ease of analysis, the feedback was segregated into 3 groupings based, on the dates of the deacons' ordinations – 1970/80s, 1990s and 2000s.

1970s/80s

I lead the following ministries…
We are consciously striving to work as a collaborative ministry team so it is perhaps incorrect to say that I 'lead'. As stated previously, I conduct funerals and weddings, I am actively involved in Baptism and wedding preparation, First Holy Communion and Confirmation programmes. I have a special relationship with the retired clergy and have over the years shared a role as an assistant chaplain to the Little Sisters of the Poor, presiding at Sunday Evening Prayer and Benediction. I am involved with weekly Eucharistic visits to the housebound and sick. I participate in the RCIA programme. I conduct services of the word with Holy Communion and act as chaplain to the Council of the Knights of St Columba which more recently is expanding to encompass the burgeoning Apostleship of the Sea in our area. I am a part of our Stewardship Leadership Team, generating and 'infecting' stewardship throughout our Parish.
Reader, Eucharistic Ministry and hospital visitors
I don't really lead any ministries except Fathers Prayers, but I do help with Knights of St Columba, and St Vincent de Paul, as chaplain. I conduct all the weddings and convalidations and help with applications for annulment. Share in the baptism programme. Jointly lead the R.C.I.A. programme with the parish sister. Take

Communion to the sick and infirm. I assist at Mass on most days and join in a weekly meeting with the clergy team.
Baptism
Extraordinary Ministers of Communion, Baptism preparation
Morning Prayer of the Church, marriage preparation programme, lay ministers of Communion, readers, visiting the housebound/sick.
In collaboration with a woman solicitor and theologian we lead biblical studies and sacramental instruction. I lead groups to cooperate in building communities with a shared church (Roman Catholic/Church of England) and also in a rural area where we rent a Church of England church for liturgical celebrations. I have been made pastorally responsible for this rural area.
I was in charge of the ministers of the Eucharist (29) for ten years. Handed it over – delegated – but available for advice.
As a retired deacon I am not involved in any particular "leadership", except that, whenever possible, I read Morning Prayer before Mass on Mondays and Fridays.
I do little now except preach at weekends
I retired from active ministry when I reached the age of 75 – but am still expected to preach and participate in the local diocesan liturgy when possible.
Baptism course
Parish altar servers & ministers of Holy Communion, *Unity* representatives. deanery bereavement care team. I am chairman of the parish liturgy committee. I have taken a leading role in the adult formation sessions which we run in the parish alternating with our PP.

Other things I would like to do but feel unable to…
Although I fully appreciate and understand that this is inconsistent with diaconal orders and the sacrament, were there a way that deacons might administer a sacrament of anointing – perhaps combined with a 'confession of desire' I think this could be something that would contribute positively to the diaconal ministry of charity.
I have enough responsibilities.
Organise and lead healing services and *Life in the Spirit* seminars.
Run a bible study course, adult education programme, follow-up to RCIA Programme, restart a bereavement group, start a group to welcome lapsed Catholics back to the Church, prayer and rosary groups, social groups to build up the community
To contribute towards a better understanding of the future of the diaconal role, taking into account the sign of the times.
No. I have no regrets.

I feel I am most a deacon when…
I baptise, do marriages, do funeral services (when there is no Requiem Mass), bless houses, consulted on annulment possibility.
I walk with people in the sacramental moments of their lives. I find marriage preparation can at times be truly inspiring, particularly when you witness the awakening awareness of God's presence in couples. From time to time this comes to the fore when sharing time

with the bereaved and so often in visiting elderly people in their homes with Holy Communion. It is perhaps the most fulfilling, privileged and awesome aspect of ministry.
I am with the people and, in particular, with the sick and the dying.
I feel I am most a deacon when I am leading the people in prayer and praise and helping them to experience the power of the Holy Spirit in their lives and to surrender their lives to God.
I assist at Mass and homiletics.
I am proclaiming the Gospel at Mass.
I am interacting with groups and being able to make them feel part of the parish community. Able to draw the 3 communities (3 Mass centres/churches) into one parish – still working on this.
I see other people taking responsibility and control of various functions within the Church as a result of the encouragement I have given to them.
I deacon at Mass. Preach the homily once a month and especially when I prepare people for marriage and baptism, and prepare people for the ceremonies of the Church. Also visiting the bereaved and preparing for funerals
I ask for the priest's blessing before reading the Gospel (and preaching of course).
I am talking to people after Mass and visiting them in their homes.
I help people get back into relationships with God and the Church, in whatever form that takes which is appropriate for them.
I am working face to face with people – one to one or couples, explaining, demythologising, comforting and teaching. In crisis times – preparing people for funerals and post-funeral visits. Liturgically – when I preach as I do regularly or officiate at Baptisms and weddings.
I carry out my threefold ministry

Areas of unmet pastoral need for this group include being able to administer a form of sacramental anointing which recognises the limitation of the deacon with regard to reconciling penitents. Such a pastoral intervention could arguably provide comfort and the sign value of Holy Orders without encroaching on the role of the priest in the forgiveness of sin and the Sacrament of the Sick. However, there may be confusion, particularly for those who are seriously ill and frail who may misconstrue the ministrations of the deacon as those of the priest.

In summary, it is clear that this group of deacons value and cherish their sacramental and liturgical roles and recognise their graced privilege of being a sacramental presence to those who are sick, bereaved or in crisis. There are similar resonances in the accounts given by the 1990s cohort, whose statements on leadership are given below.

1990s

I lead the following ministries…
Sick, Baptism.
RCIA.
Holy Communion and Readers.
I don't "lead" anything.
Baptism, altar servers training, readers.
I would prefer to say that "I SUPPORT" the following ministries: lay ministers of Communion, readers, welcomers, Justice and Peace Group, Confirmation catechists, bereavement support workers.
Monthly Benediction. Part of baptismal preparation.
Word – Communion.
I am Director of the Permanent Diaconate in the Diocese. In the parish, I lead on various parts of the First Holy Communion programme – RCIA.
Readers and Eucharistic ministers.
Eucharistic Ministry, Confirmation, Ignatian spirituality.
I don't lead any ministries: the PP is the leader.
Marriage preparation, Confirmation preparation
Liturgy of the word.
Word, sick, Baptism, Marriage.
RCIA, altar servers, marriage prep.
I am available for whatever needs to be done.
Readers, Sunday hospital visiting, marriage preparation, service of word and Holy Communion.

Other things I would like to do but feel unable to…
Communicate more effectively with youngsters.
Nothing.
Nowadays, the content and balance of my diaconate are about right for what I can manage.
As I am (X) years old and should have retired I am (over the moon) being able to do so many things and being called to do many things.
Play music well!
I am not in active ministry at the moment.
Being married, I can only give a certain amount of time to the Church; thus I have to spread my time as evenly as possible.
Leading First Communion instruction.

Baptising Babies and Clearing Gutters

Sing.
Be better informed as regards pastoral issues. I have to work full-time to provide for family. Not enough time and the cost and loss of earnings- big factor.
With the skills that I possess, being always truthful when I cannot help, but always willing to support others find the answer.
Now retired – ill health and wife with stroke.

I feel I am most a deacon when...
I visit the sick, visit the bereaved, visit parents of children preparing for Baptism.
I proclaim the gospel and preach. Also when I share my faith.
I conduct a funeral/Baptism.
I give the needy my undivided attention.
I am with people and not just in church. I am very conscious of my role among people when at work also.
I am sharing in individuals' suffering and life issues.
When I am hospital chaplain and when preaching.
I am preaching.
I serve God by my words or actions and make his love and mercy known to people.
I am with the sick or involved in the liturgy.
I am ministering to the sick and housebound and concelebrating Mass or the sacraments. (Note: although the respondent has used the term "concelebrate" he possibly intended "participate in the celebration" as only those in priestly orders may concelebrate Mass.)
I am working in the community ecumenically i.e. counselling, visiting.
I am visiting the housebound and fulfilling the liturgical role.
I never have any such feeling.
When I am not a deacon.
A role as a deacon is required. I have to divide my time with my family, work and other interests.
Pray more.
I preach, celebrate a Sacrament, console the sick/dying.
I realise that as a person I am being used by the Lord to do his work.
I take Communion to sick in hospital

Three respondents in this group challenged the use of the word "lead", one preferring the more collaborative "support", whilst another indicated that the parish priest was the "leader". Like their colleagues from the previous decade, this group found their ministry to the sick and housebound fulfilling and relevant. Two respondents, however, gave a more ambiguous response to this question; one stated that he felt he was most a deacon when he was not a deacon, whilst another pointed to the multifaceted roles he undertook at home, work and the Church, indicating that there was a need for him to subdivide his time to accommodate all of these appropriately. This was echoed by two other respondents, one of whom expressed discomfiture at the financial impact of undertaking diaconal ministry, describing this as "a big factor".

2000s

I lead the following ministries…
I train new Eucharistic ministers.
Adult formation, especially RCIA, social justice and concerns issues, liturgical formation. p.s. often support and initiate rather than lead.
Liturgy of word and Communion at airport. House group.
"Lead"? I'm involved in a variety of activities, from RCIA to Justice and Peace, to preparing the joint ecumenical service when it's our turn, to organising the day for Extraordinary Ministers of Holy Communion, giving sessions on the social teaching etc etc.
RCIA, Confirmation, candidates in formation, faith development.
I try to ensure each ministry area has catechists and a co-ordinator rather than lead them myself; then I provide training and support to the leader and group.
The ministry of the administration of the temporal goods of the Church.

Other things I would like to do but feel unable to…
More theological formation of parish. Evangelisation work. Work with young people. Visiting sick and others.
Time restricts my teaching/formation role.
I know it is not possible but anointing will always involve the PP to visit as well.
Be present at funerals more often.
At the moment I'm restricted by being in full-time employment. I would very much like to expand my activities more into deanery and diocesan activities appropriate to my ministry, experience and education.
I am getting too old to relate effectively to children. I can't sing or direct musical side of liturgy.
Oh so much…everywhere I turn there are possibilities. We have no youth group, no SVP, no scripture group, no welcoming ministry – the work is plentiful but for willing souls to do it.

I feel I am most a deacon when …
I talk to unmarried parents about marriage without alienating them.
I get up in the morning i.e. I think all the time in and out of Church environment.
I catechise, work with marginalised, listen.
I minister at airport, at Mass, weddings, Baptisms, funerals. Visit sick and needy. Fraternals and services.
I am being talked at by someone.
I am a "deacon" all the time – that's my calling – available to do what God and the Church call me to do.
I kneel during the Consecration.
I am visiting the dying, sick, those in pain or crisis, and accompanying them as a fellow Christian and as a minister. For community to work, it has to have a visible face, who knows the person and becomes present when it counts.
I pray the Divine Office for the Church and the world, preach the gospel, serve the bishop and the wider diocese in my diocesan role.

Like their colleagues in the earlier groups, the 2000s cohort undertook a full range of catechetical and formation duties and valued their role in ministry to the sick. One alluded to the anointing of the sick by the parish priest and although fully accepted this unique priestly role, like his colleague in the 1970/80s cohort, would perhaps welcome the institution of a diaconal anointing which could be a sign of healing rather than sacramental forgiveness.

Two respondents regarded themselves as deacons at all times and saw no dichotomy between their secular and family roles and their sacred ministry, although three respondents mentioned the restricted time which they could devote to ministry because of other responsibilities. Perhaps the most self-effacing statement was from the respondent who felt most a deacon when he was "being talked at by someone". In terms of pastoral deficits, one respondent listed a variety of needs in his parish including provision for the poor (St Vincent de Paul), youth ministry, welcome ministry and scripture formation.

For personal reflection or for discussion in small groups

1. How does the deacon's leadership complement the leadership of the priest in your parish?

2. How can the deacon encourage gifted lay leadership in the parish?

Endnotes

---

[1] http://www.catholicculture.org/culture/library/dictionary/index.cfm?id=36430 accessed 20/01/2012

[2] Although De Pree's context was originally the office furniture company Herman Millar, an institute bearing his name was set up at Fuller Theological Seminary, Pasadena, California.

[3] De Pree, M. "Servant –Leadership: Three Things Necessary" in Spears, L.C. and M. Lawrence (eds) 2002 Focus *on Leadership: Servant Leadership for the Twenty-First Century.* New York: John Wiley and Sons. p.91.

[4] Ibid p.92.

[5] Kasper, W. 2003. *Leadership in the Church.* New York: Crossroad. p.21.

7 | WHAT DO DEACONS ACTUALLY DO?

We know from the earlier chapters what deacons are permitted by canon law to undertake. Their role as "ordinary ministers" of Holy Communion, administering infant Baptisms, officiating at weddings and funerals are clear. However, how do deacons actually spend much of their ministerial time?

Range of diaconal ministries

Unlike the previous chapter which explored the leadership of deacons and asked them to nominate the ministries which they led, in this question, deacons were invited to name all the ministries in which they were actually involved. This ensured that roles not directly related to Holy Orders e.g. civic and inter-faith roles were included. The responses are presented in three tranches- 1970s/80s, 1990s and 2000s. In order to minimise duplication, pastoral support roles to external organisations have been included but those for hospitals, schools and prisons are dealt with under "Chaplaincy".

"External" Diaconal Ministries

1970s/1980s
Sub-group Christian Unity Ecumenical Development Group, CAFOD, Wells for India, various Advent and Lenten Appeals – changes every year.
I was for several years the chairman of the X Town and District Christian Council and have coordinated the Clergy Prayer Breakfasts until recently. I remain part of the planning group for joint celebrations in X district. I serve on the County Unity Commission.
Inter-denominational role and charitable role.
Royal Naval association, within the hospital and service organisation, chaplain to Knights of St Columba (X Town Council), chaplain to Royal Naval Association (Y Branch) member of the British Legion.
I lead Fathers Prayers, an international organisation… and it is spreading in a number of countries, including Australia and New Zealand.

None of these high profile roles are available in a semi-rural environment.
Police chaplaincy.
Christians Together (in Town X), South London Industrial Mission (SLIM) RC Member.
I have maintained an involvement with Christians Together in X through a variety of ecumenical activities Prayer Groups, Lenten Programmes, Joint Overseas Aid Projects and Civic activities. I maintain a relationship with both the Muslim and Jewish communities attending their Festivals and including them in appropriate activities where possible i.e. Catenian Clergy nights. Charitable roles – Christian Aid, CAFOD. Early in my Ministry I was involved as an assistant to the prison chaplaincy. I have maintained some involvement in aftercare in collaboration with the SVP.
Borough Dean, inter-faith forum, SVP, Knights of St Columba.

1990s
Apostleship of the Sea Port Chaplain
Churches Together in X town, Catholic Children's Society, Treasurer of *Churches Together* in Y Area (Ecumenism)
Church charity shop, social group.
Churches Together
Chaplain Knights of St Columba
County Ecumenical Officer (a part-time salaried post for *Churches Together* in X County)
Lead a group of mainly retired ministers of other faiths. Membership of 25.
Lead a small charismatic prayer group (Interfaith)
CAFOD, Augustinian Sierra Leone Mission.
Interdenominational – building relationships between our churches.
Bereavement/funerals, leading adults to faith.
MENCAP. Chaplain to the local ambulance station.
Interdenominational and inter-faith, CAFOD and J&P. Please note that I have been involved in all these things, but less so now.
Minor role in ecumenical pilgrimage organisation.
Churches Together. Support others in their work.

2000s
Involved with the *Maranatha* Community.
Represent parish clergy on *Churches Together* Charitable roles e.g. *Christian Aid*, CAFOD etc. Organise *Christian Aid* on behalf of the parish
Clergy Fraternals and *Churches Together*.
Airport, villages, Justice &Peace and St Vincent de Paul. Admin, finance
Chair of the *Churches Together* for 3 years- now ending.
CAFOD, Justice &Peace.
Churches Together

What Do Deacons Actually Do?

As the above table indicates, the deacons are visible witnesses in the community in ways which would, perhaps, be difficult for the parish priest. The 1990s and 2000s deacons would appear to be less active in the areas of Justice and Peace, but it is likely that their professional and family commitments, together with their liturgical and sacramental duties, render further pastoral outreach impossible.

Sacramental preparation

The feedback from the deacons indicates that their key areas of ministry are, not surprisingly, sacramental preparation and liturgical functions. As the histogram illustrates, preparation for and officiating at the rites of Baptism and Marriage are the dominant ministries in which the deacons of Southwark Province are engaged (30.2% and 35.8% respectively).

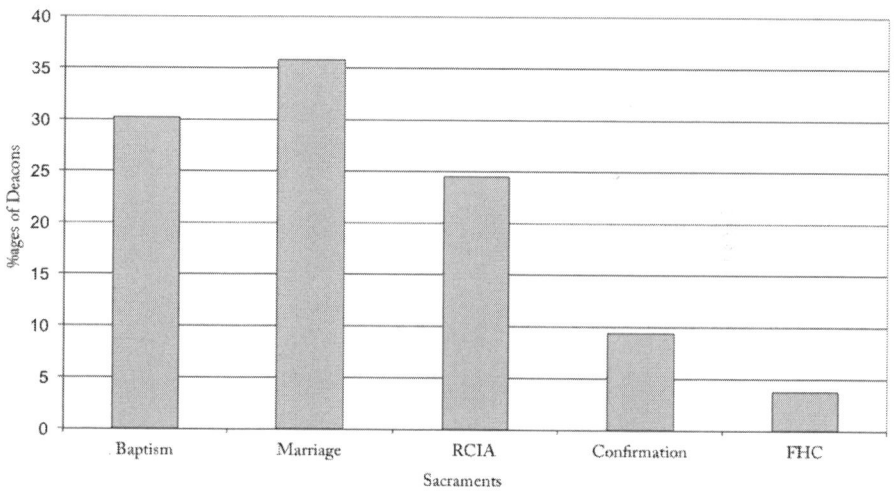

Sacramental Roles for Deacons

Diaconal Ministry in Sacramental Rites and Preparation

RCIA (Rite of Christian Initiation of Adults) is also a key area for deacons, with 24.5% engaged in this specific adult formation. Sacramental preparation of children and young people i.e. Confirmation and First Holy Communion is, however, not a key area of diaconal ministry, with 9.4% and 3.8% declaring involvement in these respective roles. This may reflect the mature age of the deacons or there may, perhaps, be gender issues, particularly in the care of very young children.

Diaconal Chaplaincy

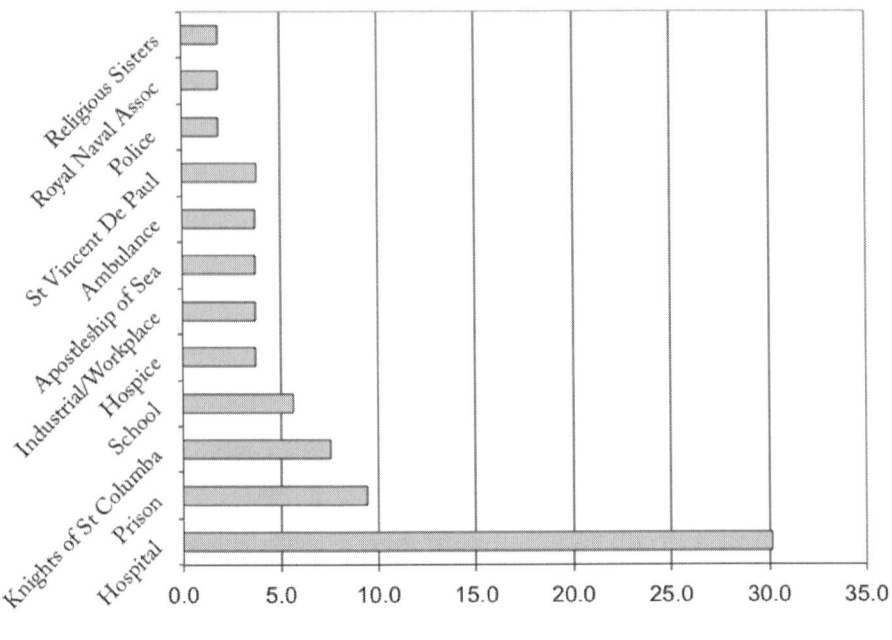

%ages of deacons

Diaconal Chaplaincy

Diaconal chaplaincy is undertaken for a wide range of clients with the highest proportion i.e. 30.2% carried out in a hospital setting. 9.4%, and 5.7% minister in prisons and schools respectively whilst 3.8% provide pastoral care to hospices, the Ambulance Service, *Apostleship of the Sea*, the Society of St Vincent de Paul and in occupational and industrial settings. A small minority of 1.9% minister to a community of religious sisters with the same percentage serving the Police Force and the Royal Naval Association. The largest voluntary and charitable sector served by deacons is the Order of the Knights of St Columba with 7.5% of deacons ministering to this group.

Ministry to the Eucharistic Assembly

Although the deacon's major liturgical role at Mass relates to the proclamation of the Gospel and in delivering the homily, when permitted to do so, the term "ministry of the word" may also be validly applied to catechesis. In order to avoid ambiguity, the term "ministry to the Eucharistic assembly" will be used to designate the deacon's role at Mass i.e. proclaiming the gospel and breaking open the word in the homily. 73.6% of respondents are involved in proclaiming the gospel and preaching, although it cannot be inferred that those who proclaim the gospel also deliver the homily. One respondent, although now retired from active ministry, still continues to "preach and participate in the local diocesan liturgy when possible" whilst another preaches one weekend in four and another, four to six times per year. It is a role which some find demanding but is, nonetheless, cherished by those who perform this duty as an "honour and humility to pronounce the word of God in the gospel and attempt to open this up to the congregation" (Respondent 362).

Funerals and support to the bereaved and distressed

32% of respondents to the study indicated that they take an active role in funeral services – the preparation of the service, the rite itself and bereavement support afterwards. The Ushaw findings shown in the table below indicate that 33.9% of deacons preside at funerals about once a month with 41.1% presiding less than monthly although 3.6% do so on a weekly basis and a further 5.4% preside more than weekly.

Baptising Babies and Clearing Gutters

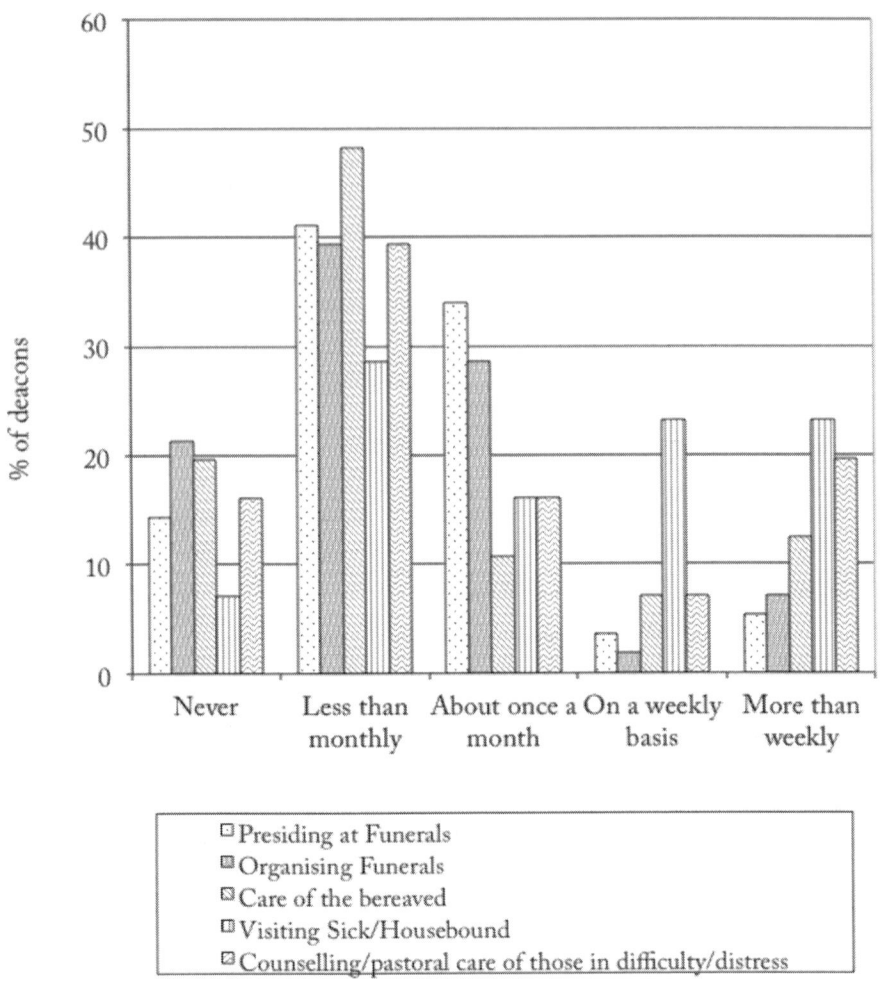

Diaconal Ministry to the Dying, Bereaved,
the sick and those who are distressed (Ushaw Study 2007)

The overall findings of the Ushaw Study

The 2007 Ushaw study[1] on the permanent diaconate in England and Wales focused on the levels of emotional exhaustion or satisfaction in ministry and concluded that deacons reported higher levels of both satisfaction and exhaustion in ministry than full-time members of the clergy. The deacons who reported higher satisfaction in ministry felt valued, saw themselves as members of the clergy, frequently undertook a range of ministerial activities and were in full-time employment. Those who had higher levels of emotional exhaustion did not feel valued, performed significant roles seldom or never, had a poor relationship with their parish priest and lower levels of spirituality.[2] Extracted data from this study, relating to the 56 respondents from Southwark Province, show a range of ministry activities consistent with the findings of the present study. The tables below indicate the time devoted to a range of duties. These have been presented in chart format under the titles "Sacramental Preparation", "Ministry of the Word", "Death and Bereavement, Sick and Distressed", "Chaplaincy" and "Other Works of Charity". Whilst there is inevitably some crossover in the ministry provided i.e. chaplaincy and sacramental preparation will include some ministry of the word, the classifications reflect those used in the Ushaw Study questionnaire. The Ushaw findings offer a quantitative account of diaconal ministry through a series of questions which invited deacons to specify the amount of time devoted to specific ministries. Although the response rate from the Southwark cohort in the Ushaw study is not dissimilar to the present study i.e. 56 respondents to the Ushaw research and 53 to the present study, there can be no direct inference that the respondents are the same, although the profiles of the respondents are similar and the total population of interest is of course the same.

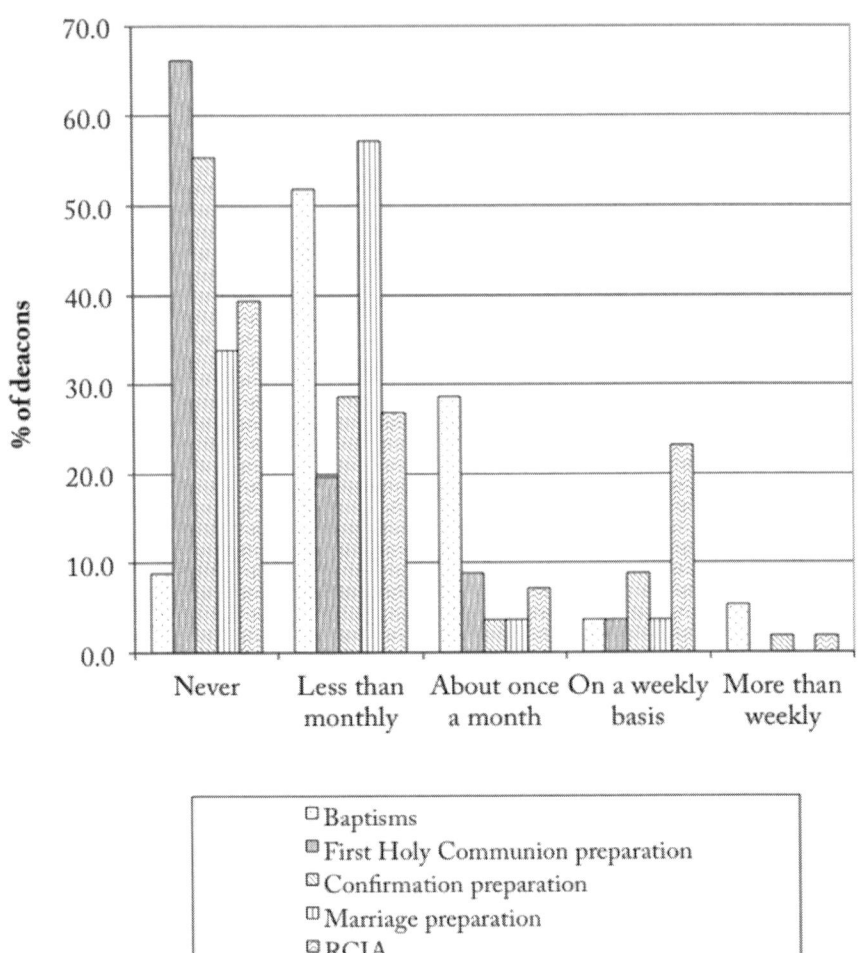

Diaconal Ministry for Sacramental Preparation (Ushaw Study 2007)

| What Do Deacons Actually Do?

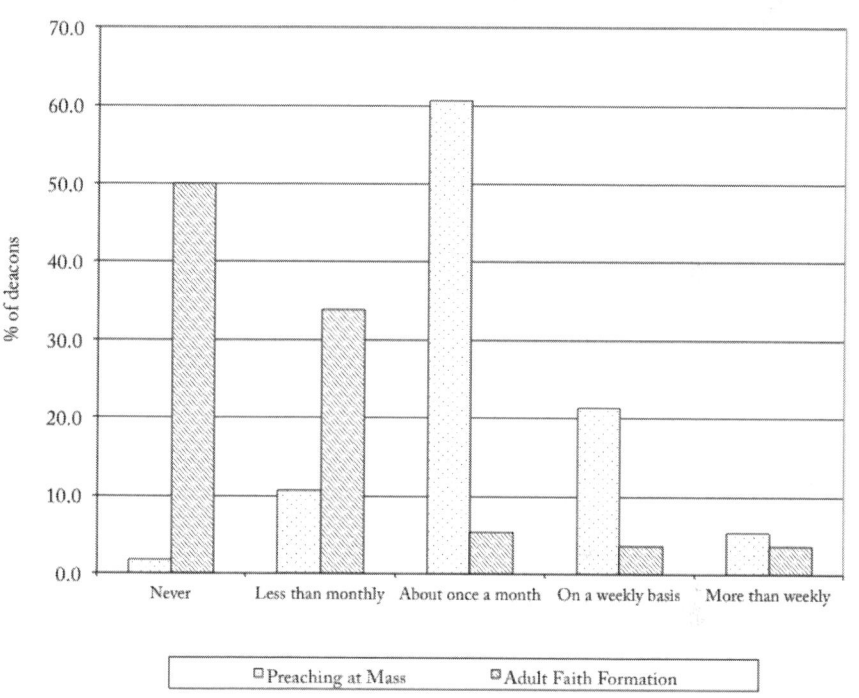

Diaconal Ministry of the Word (Ushaw Study 2007)

Baptising Babies and Clearing Gutters

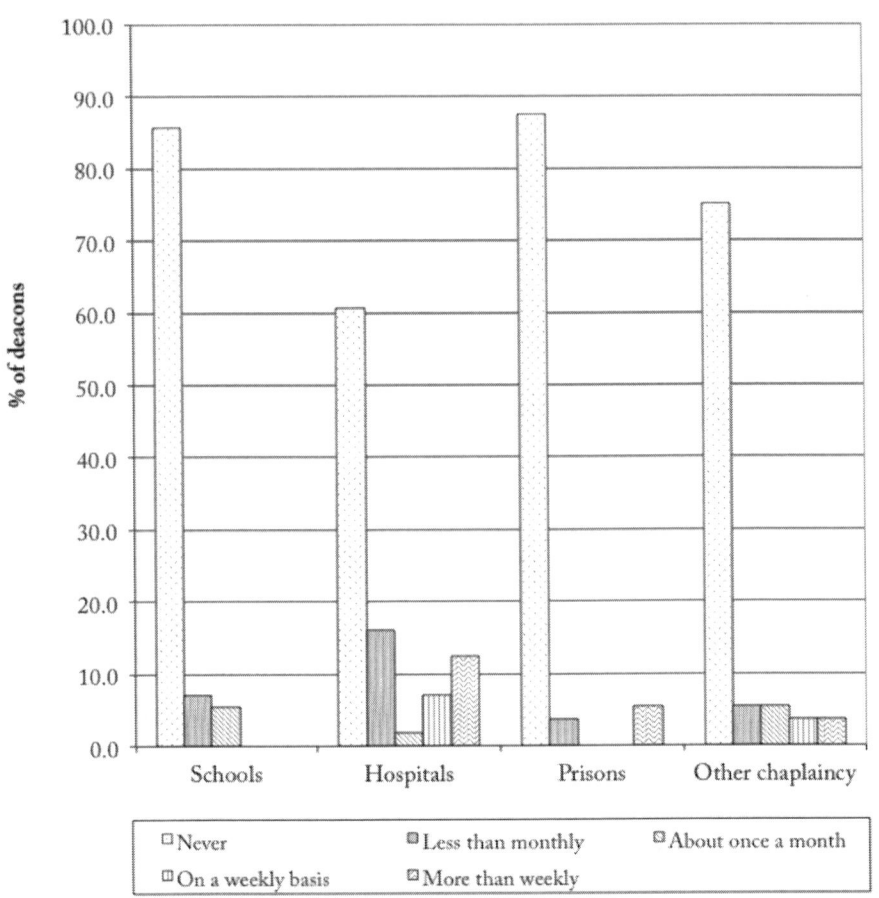

Diaconal Chaplaincy (Ushaw Study 2007)

| What Do Deacons Actually Do?

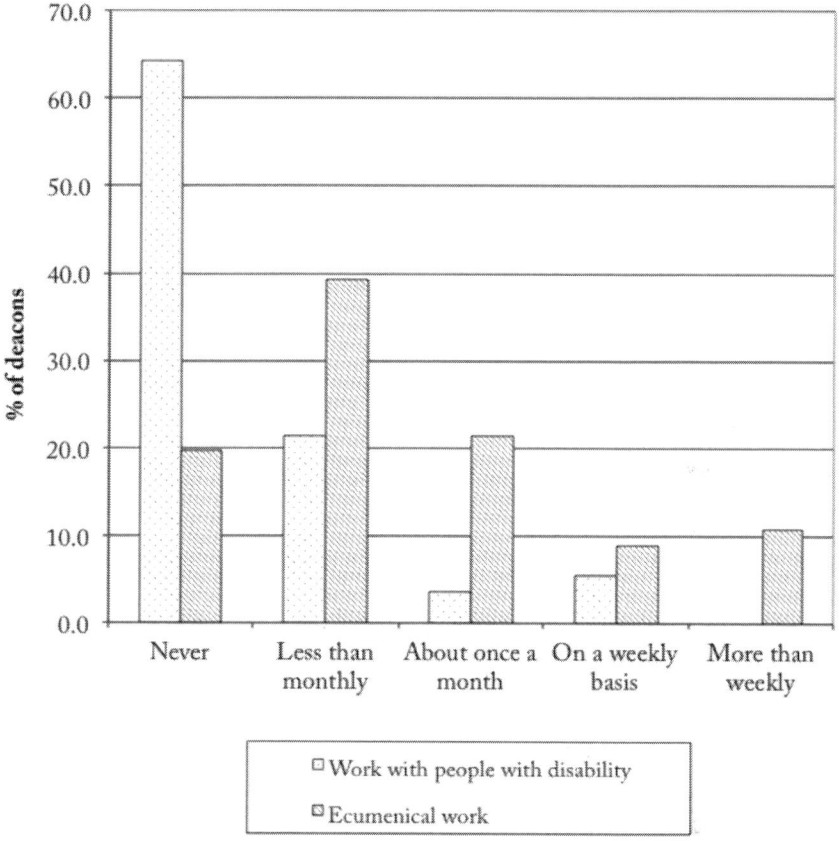

Other Diaconal Works of Charity (Ushaw Study 2007)

The Ushaw findings indicate that, like the Southwark Province study, the key sacramental roles for the deacon relate to Baptism, Marriage and RCIA. 28.6% of deacons are engaged "about once per month" in activities related to the Rite of Baptism whilst 51.8% report their involvement in this ministry as "less than monthly". Similarly, marriage preparation is undertaken by 57.1% of deacons "less than monthly" although a small minority report activity in this ministry "about once a month" (3.6%) or "on a weekly basis" (3.6%). RCIA would appear to present the most consistent time demand for deacons in the area of sacramental preparation with 23.2% declaring weekly involvement in this ministry. The Ushaw outcomes for Confirmation and First Holy Communion programmes endorse the Southwark Province findings that these sacraments are not areas of major involvement for permanent deacons with 66.1% declaring that they are never involved in First Holy Communion preparation and 55.4% never engaged in Confirmation programmes.

The Ushaw study indicates that 60.7% of deacons preach at Mass on a monthly basis and 21.4% do so weekly. Analysis of the narrative accounts of the deacons' ministry of the word in the Southwark Province study indicates that 73.6% of deacons are involved in proclaiming the gospel and delivering homilies. The differences in these findings may be a result of the emphasis placed on the preaching role by the individual deacons. The Ushaw study invited a quantitative response based on frequency whilst the Southwark Province study invited narrative responses to the two "leadership" statements "I lead the following ministries…." And "I feel I am most a deacon when…." and a question which invited respondents to name which of the diaconal ministries (word, sacrament and charity) most suited their personality and giftedness. Both approaches to this issue have their merits and their limitations. The quantitative approach may imply a value, based upon time spent, whilst the qualitative approach may simply render a timeframe impossible to determine e.g. an occasional homily, carefully crafted and delivered may be pastorally more significant than routine mediocre accounts which are delivered on a weekly basis. Conversely, an experienced and gifted homilist may be a liturgical high spot in an otherwise uninspiring liturgy.

For personal reflection or for discussion in small groups

1. Which areas of ministry do you most associate with <u>your</u> parish deacon?
2. Which other areas of need (if any) would you like him to address either directly or indirectly?
3. What are the advantages and disadvantages of deploying deacons as chaplains in hospitals, schools and prisons?

Endnotes

---

[1] Geary, B and Kendall, J. 2007. "The Diaconate in Scotland, England and Wales: A Demographic Profile and an Investigation of Well-being and Diaconal Identity". Paper presented at Ushaw Bicentennial Colloquium: *Formation for the Future- Discovering Mutually Receptive Gifts*. Durham, England. January 2008

[2] Ushaw Report p.1. Although the term "lower levels of spirituality" is a highly subjective term and might appear judgemental, this is the terminology used by the Ushaw researchers and reflects the responses given by their research participants and is outside the scope of this author's work.

In proclaiming the Gospel at Mass, the deacon undertakes the mandate given to him at ordination —"Receive the Gospel of Christ, whose herald you now are. Believe what you read, teach what you believe, and practise what you teach."

The deacon articulates the incarnational prayer at the mingling of the water and wine at the Offertory of the Mass:. "By the mystery of this water and wine, may we come to share in the divinity of Christ, who humbled himself to share in our humanity." See page 142

At the end of the Service of Word and Holy Communion, Deacon Stephen prepares the pyx for bringing Holy Communion to a housebound parishioner.

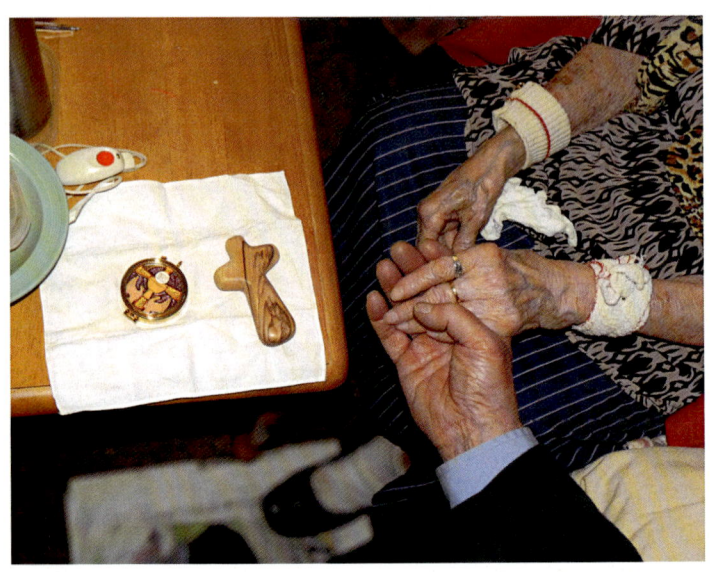

The deacon's ministry to the housebound and frail ensures that these members of the Body of Christ are not neglected or forgotten. These are today's Hellenist widows mentioned in Acts 6.

*Deacon Stephen prepares young candidates for
the Sacrament of Reconciliation*

*Many deacons are involved in chaplaincy roles in schools, prisons and
hospitals. Deacon Anthony, a member of the chaplaincy team in a major
London hospital, ministers to patients, staff and visitors.*

Deacon Roger, a chaplain with the Apostleship of the Sea, on board an oil tanker berthed at Southampton.
Photograph courtesy of BBC South, 'Sea City' © BBC

In welcoming new members into the people of God through Baptism, the deacon can be seen as a "minister of the threshold."

8 | WHAT DEACONS FEEL ABOUT THEIR MINISTRY

In this set of questions, the deacons were invited to reflect on the gains and losses they experienced as a result of their ministerial life, specifically:

What do you value most in being a deacon? What losses (if any) do you associate with being a deacon?

Of the 17 deacons ordained in the 1970s and 80s, one declined to answer both questions and another gave a nil response to the first question. 7 respondents (41.2%) reported no losses associated with their diaconal ministry. The remaining respondents listed the following:

- Loss of leisure time and hobbies x 4
- Inability to make spontaneous decisions to go out with the family x 2
- Unable to say "no" to the Church and family suffered
- Inability "to be incognito within the confines of the town"
- Loss of professional progress
- "Children missed out when I spent more time as a deacon and not so much as a husband/father"

The majority of respondents expressed their value in terms of service to the People of God and the Church, helping people to get closer to God and in "opening up matters of faith and belief". In terms of their own personal gain, one respondent felt that the diaconate was "very much my life" and another that "I am achieving something of my aspiration for personal spirituality…my relationship with God is deepened and become real, so much so that there are times, I trust without presumption, when I dare to look forward with excitement to the 'next great adventure' – eternal life!!"

Of the 22 deacons in the group ordained in the 1990s, there were 2 "nil responses" to both of the questions and a further 6 respondents (27.2%) who left the question on losses unanswered. A further 8 respondents (36.3%) stated that they had no losses associated with their ministry. However, 5 respondents (22.7%) highlighted adverse impact on their family lives, with 3 stating that their ministry had created difficulty in their marriages.

Among the aspects valued by this cohort were "helping others", "serving the parish", and "being drawn closer to Our Lord in the process of ministering to others". 3 respondents highlighted the importance of Holy Orders to their service – "a real source of strength" (Respondent 393) as "a formal witness as a person who is a tool in the hand of Our Lord Jesus Christ" (Respondent 300) and "being the presence of Jesus to others in a sacramental sense" (Respondent 317).

Of the 14 deacons ordained in the 2000s, one declined to answer the question about any losses associated with his ministry whilst 4 (28.6%) could not nominate anything which they would consider a loss. 7 respondents (50%) mentioned lack of availability for family, with 1 respondent specifically aware of lack of time with his wife. Another highlighted the separation from his wife when he undertook duties at the altar. One respondent in this group alluded to his public profile in ordained ministry, feeling himself to be now "public property". This re-echoes the views of one of his peers in the 1980s group who was no longer able to be "incognito in the town". Two wry observations were included in the losses section – "Freedom to choose whether to get up for morning Mass on Sunday!" and "I can no longer be dissolute, but that is a gain." The overwhelming value associated with their diaconate was the charism of service with 7 respondents (50%) expressing the joy of "giving time to people" or "being 'there' for people". Others expressed their service in more theological terminology e.g. "Being ontologically changed" (Respondent 368), "Being engaged in a permanent, public and sacramental way in the building up of the Kingdom"

(Respondent 420), "Having an extra channel of grace to communicate the Holy Spirit to people i.e. by the grace of ordination" (Respondent 498). Rootedness in the faith community was also identified as significant e.g. "The attachment to a community of people who worship together and being part of the ordained ministry is humbling" (Respondent 445) and "The support and prayer of all those around me and then being able to reciprocate" (Respondent 399).

In summary, the responses of all three cohorts were characterised by a humble recognition of being called to serve in a way which sometimes entails real personal sacrifice and detriment to the family life of the deacon. These themes were further explored in the section of the questionnaire entitled "Life at home/work".

Life at home/work

The questions in this section have again been segregated into 3 groups, reflecting the decades within which the respondents were ordained, with the 1970s and 1980s being combined because of small numbers in the former category.

Describe how your vocation and ministry has impacted on your life as a married man (if applicable).

All but one of the 17 deacons of the 1970s/80s group responded to this question and, with the exception of one respondent who noted having to forego leisure time because of the needs of other people, the impact on married life by their ministry was generally positive. The support of wives and their selflessness in accommodating their husbands' ministry were noted by 10 respondents (58.8%). One stated that his diaconal calling had not impacted on his life as a married man, but rather, that his life as a married man had impacted on his vocation and ministry. Several respondents cherished the forbearance of their wives in fitting family outings and holidays around the deacon's parish commitments and also for their spouses' pastoral support in taking telephone messages and welcoming visitors connected to their husbands' ministry into their homes. Two respondents were mindful that their vocation within marriage took precedence over their ordination, with one stating that his wife is a "person, not an appendage" to his ministry. It was also noted that some deacons' wives undertook pastoral ministry in their own right, including RCIA catechesis, editing a parish directory and involvement in a Christian Unity Commission.

Of those ordained in the 1990s, one respondent designated this question "not applicable", 2 declined to provide a response, whilst a further 2 stated that that their ministry had no impact on their lives as married men. The remaining 16 deacons within this group (72.7%) listed a range of both adverse and positive effects. There was a realisation of significant time pressures, resulting in the curtailment of family activities. Respondents noted that they needed to proactively manage time set aside for their spouses e.g. "I am fortunate to have a very supportive wife who can also be very honest with me and make me aware when I am saying 'Yes' too often. The grace of my ordination works in our married life, helping my wife and I to confront potentially difficult situations and talk them through before things get silly" (Respondent 393). Two respondents acknowledged that their ministry had put a strain on their marriages. On a more positive note, however, some found that ministry heightened their awareness of the needs of their spouses, and that this had led to happier and more fulfilled marriages. One respondent spoke of how the joy of his marriage enabled him to help others (Respondent 417) and another noted that the process of formation and subsequent ordained ministry had brought his wife and himself closer together, both as a couple and in their respective ministries within the Church. Respondent 300 recalled that his bishop had cautioned him about achieving the correct balance between his marriage and his diaconate, with the former being his prime commitment. This advice had been well received and the deacon saw his ministry as a "development of the person as a tool of the Lord and, as such, it enhances both married and family life."

In the 2000s group, one respondent registered "Not Applicable" to this question but the remaining 13 deacons in this group offered their reflections, 5 of whom highlighted the negative impact of ministry on married life (35.7%). One respondent noted that he and his wife had found it difficult to balance their family life and Church life and that the marriage had come under strain – "The

Church took over my life for five years and I lived in a sort of artificial 'demi-monde'. I am now firmly back in the 'real' world and everything is a lot better and my ministry is more enjoyable". One respondent spoke of the sacrifice for his family and his wife, who was now deceased, and another that he and his wife "both need to watch our youngest child doesn't get dragged along too much". Other respondents, whilst noting the tensions which were brought to bear on family life by diaconal ministry expressed their appreciation of their awareness in this regard: "All for the good. I have had to work harder at being mindful of my wife's need for family time. Made that voice of my conscience all the more loud" (Respondent 399), and "I am fortunate to have a wife who is as committed to serving God as I am. We are able to share the highs (and the lows) that this service brings. I hope that I have become more appreciative of her love and support as a result of my vocation and ministry" (Respondent 362).

Describe how your vocation has impacted on your life as a family man (if applicable)

3 of the 17 respondents from the 1970s/80s group (17.6%) declined to answer this question. Of the remaining 14 respondents, 8 (57.1%) were positive about the impact of their ministry on family life although 2 noted that their children had already left home during the period of the formation and their subsequent life as ordained ministers.

Some respondents felt that their family life had been helped or "completed" by their diaconal ministry and others spoke of their liturgical role in major family events e.g. officiating at the funerals of parents, the marriages of their children and the baptisms of their grandchildren. Negative comments related to time pressures placed on families by diaconal duties, and two respondents reported that their children had been adversely affected at school, with teachers or peers expecting them to be "models of virtue". This phenomenon has also been identified in Wijngaards Serrarens' 2006 research on the experiences of the wives of deacons. She notes that deacons' families may feel very much at the centre of public attention and that "model behaviour could thus be expected". Participants in this

Dutch study spoke of "the family living in a goldfish bowl" and "Some people think we are super beings that never have conjugal or family problems (or are not allowed to have these!) Essentially, our children should be perfect."[1] Cummings account of this "exemplarism" goes even further to include the pressure which the deacon himself may impose on his own family to become a "flagship of familial propriety and domestic perfection." Cummings notes that exemplarism is grossly unfair to both the deacon and his family as it imposes unrealistic expectations upon them all. "The *deacon* was ordained, *not* his family."[2]

There were 2 nil responses from the 1990s group to this question and an additional 4 for whom the question was not applicable. Like their earlier peers, the time pressure placed on families by diaconal ministry was noted by 11 respondents (50%). Mention was made of the tolerance of wives and children – "our children are mercifully, lovely adults. Their dad is their dad and they understand him and have been very supportive!" (Respondent 482), "The Church has always been a large part of my life and as far as they are concerned, the main difference now is that occasionally I put on a Roman collar" (Respondent 393). One respondent had taken early retirement from work at the beginning of his studies for the ministry and gave up part-time work on ordination, thereby minimising the impact of his ministry on family life.

Within the 2000s group, there were 2 "nil returns" and a further response of "not applicable". The remaining 11 respondents (79%) offered nuanced reflections about the impact of their ministry on their families. 3 reported that their children simply perceived their father's ministry as "just Dad doing his Church work" (Respondent 442), "they have always taken my ministry as part of the 'me' they know (Respondent 490) and another "My children are grown up and very pleased that their dad is a deacon. They always offer advice and reflection on my work which is wonderful as it is clearly 'without prejudice' and honest feedback, for example, on my homilies" (Respondent 445).

It is interesting to note that in the 1990s and 2000s cohort, there was no reference made to the type of exemplarism noted in the

1970s/80s group. This may be indicative a more realistic level of expectation in the parish community than in the early days of the restored permanent diaconate.

Describe how your vocation has impacted on your professional life (if applicable). Are your colleagues at work aware that you are in Roman Catholic Holy Orders? If so, what difference, if any, does it make?

The responses to these questions have been summarised across all age groups and cohorts since 58.5% of respondents declared themselves to be now retired or semi-retired. As has already been noted, two deacons chose to retire early from their professions, a further two reduced their working time in order to devote themselves to ministry, three changed careers entirely, one curtailed promotion prospects, and one retired in order to train for the priesthood.

From the 53 respondents across all cohorts, 7 chose not to answer the question and a further 5 returned a "Not applicable" response and it is surmised that these respondents were retired. An additional 11 declared themselves to be retired, of whom 5 declared that their ministry had not made a discernible difference to their professional lives. Other respondents however alluded to the public witness of their ministry, although they were not providing diaconal ministry in the workplace. One noted that "If anything, people trust me more. Strangely, it is non-believers, which is a bit funny", whilst another found that there was great interest in his role as a deacon, especially as he had to travel abroad extensively. Respondent 317 found that his employer was happy for him to be regarded as an unofficial chaplain and gave him time off work to do diaconal duties. Another stated that his colleagues knew and that "one of the most endearing statements that I heard was when an individual was having problems and a colleague said 'Do you want to talk to our deacon?'"

For other respondents, their ministerial identity was not officially acknowledged in the workplace. As Respondent 500 noted "My bosses knew I was heavily involved in the RC Church but I am not sure whether they understood to what extent", and Respondent 442 reported that his chief executive and line manager knew he was ordained and this was included in some personal details on the intranet, without specifying the denomination. As was noted earlier, he added that "Nowadays, this is a delicate matter, particularly for a Christian, more still for an RC Christian who is ordained." For some, there was a reserved response from some colleagues who avoided "certain speech and behaviour when they were with me" (Respondent 393), or indeed some degree of exclusion when it came to indulging in office gossip and "in-jokes" (Respondent 478). For Respondent 495 there was concern in the ranks of his senior management because "they didn't want a 'Holy Joe' approach being applied to business matters" and for Respondent 372, the lack of cooperation he experienced in the workplace came from his Roman Catholic colleagues. On the positive side, some respondents acknowledged that they were approached by colleagues for guidance and pastoral support. Respondent 317 had conducted a number of "Christian" funeral services for colleagues and their family members whilst Respondents 371 and 354 reported being asked the "awkward" questions like "Why does God allow suffering?" Perhaps the most succinct but confident response came from Respondent 356 who simply said "Yup, they love it and take the mick, but are respectful."

Clearly for those respondents who were employed in a diocesan capacity, the connection between their professional roles and their *diakonia* was explicit and visible.

In summarising this strand of the deacons' story, it is clear that men who have roles which require discernment, authority and leadership in their family and professional lives bring these riches into their *diakonia*. How they exercise servant leadership will of course differ from person to person, and the context in which they minister will require different responses. The needs, for example, of a bereaved family will differ considerably from those of a couple who are seeking convalidation of their marriage or baptism for their child. Compassion and affirmation however will be required for each and every pastoral context and the deacon, modelling himself on the sacrificial giving of Christ, will be required to minister accordingly.

For personal reflection or for discussion in small groups

1. How can the deacon be assisted by his parish so that his ministry does not adversely impact upon his marriage and his family life?
2. What is your experience of deacons in the workplace?

Endnotes

---

[1] Wijngaards Serrarens, N. 2006. *Partners in Solidarity*. Steenwiijk, Netherlands: Grafisch Productiebedrijf Gorter. p.19.

[2] Cummings, O.F. 2004. *Deacons and the Church*. New York: Paulist Press. p.111.

9 | Inviting "Theological Conversations"

The aim of this chapter is to hold an effective theological conversation between three partners – the presenting issues or experience of the deacons of Southwark Province, the Church's voice of tradition and teaching and the current social context. The purpose of the exercise is to seek a pastoral response to the original research question "What is the ecclesial understanding of the role of the permanent diaconate in the contemporary Roman Catholic Church in England and Wales, with specific reference to Southwark Province?" In this context, the deacons' experience includes their ideas, feelings and insights. The Ushaw research project, referred to earlier, provided additional valuable insights into the levels of satisfaction experienced by deacons in Southwark Province, together with quantitative summaries of the ministries in which they engage. To this valuable body of work, I now add further social scientific research to help flag up possible future developments in the ministry of the permanent deacon.

A significant research project undertaken in the Diocese of Cleveland, Ohio in 1994[1] explored the "Effects of the Ministerial Environment on Roman Catholic Permanent Deacons and their Spouses", and its results were consistent with those in Southwark Province. Latcovich's research drew responses from 204 deacons and their spouses – a return rate of over 90% and it is possible to trace parallel strands of experience in both the Diocese of Cleveland and Southwark Province in the UK.

Latcovich's findings suggested that:

> ...deacons and their wives identify themselves in traditional family roles, with strong feelings about their own impact in the Church. The role of the wife in the

diaconate takes on the traditional clergy-wife role of support. The complex nature of the environment demands great flexibility, communication and time management, since undefined family boundaries and parish expectations may affect both the deacon's ministry and marriage.[2]

Negative aspects identified by Latcovich's analysis included unrealistic expectations from pastoral staff (rather than parishioners), levels of communication between spouses and sensitivity to the inclusion of the deacon's wife as an invited guest to clergy gatherings. Latcovich highlights the significant stress to deacons when their pastors and lay ecclesial ministers assumed they would be available at every parish function. Another issue which finds resonance in Southwark Province was lack of involvement in the parish decision-making process, as meetings were held during the day when deacons were at their secular employment. In the case of the Southwark deacons, the meetings referred to by respondents tended to be clergy gatherings rather than parish meetings.

Positive effects felt by Latcovich's cohort were the parish support systems which provided friendship and affirmation. Many anticipated the findings of their UK peers in acknowledging their wives as their most loyal mainstay and support. Latcovich's findings, however, provide more than a simple means of comparing two diaconal populations. His reflection on the theological relevance of the deacon's two vocational sacraments – marriage and Holy Orders, point to an area of discourse which is still relatively uncharted.

Towards a theology of diaconal marriage

Latcovich notes that the "special charism" of service in marriage and the deep love for the Church are two traits that formation programmes consider when screening candidates for the diaconate. He points to Rahner's articulation of the theology of marriage in *The Church and the Sacraments*:

> Marriage and the covenant between God and humanity in Christ can not only be compared by us, they stand objectively in such a relationship that matrimony

objectively represents this love of God in Christ for the Church; the relation and the attitude of Christ to the Church is the model for the relation and attitude that belongs to marriage and is mirrored by imitation in marriage so the latter is something contained or involved in the former.³

Drawing on the perspective of Kasper, Latcovich then outlines the ecclesiological implications of marriage:

> Marriage and family life are in a very special sense the Church in miniature – Vatican II spoke of the family as domestic Church…They in fact make an active contribution to the building up of the Church. That is why married couples have a special charism, that is a distinctive call, gift and form of service within the Church.⁴

Many of Latcovich's respondents found that a prayer life shared with their spouses had provided a new level of spiritual communication and that spiritual formation had enhanced their marriages.⁵ Daily prayer gave deacons deeper insight, not only in their relationship with God, but also with their wives and families. Spiritual direction also had a significant effect on the way they related to their spouses and overall, their ministry gave them a spiritual energy which renewed all aspects of their lives.

Whilst there is recognition within the Southwark Province diaconate of the self-giving of the deacons' wives, and that the written permission of wives is sought as part of the screening process for aspirants to the diaconate, there is little evidence that there is a developed theology of marriage in relation to the diaconate within formation programmes. There are, for example, fewer opportunities for UK deacon's wives to be theologically formed in relation to their husband's ministry than many of their peers in the USA, who are invited to attend the entire diaconal formation and training programme with their spouses.⁶ Also the concept of a "diaconal couple" has not yet appeared to have taken root within the UK diaconate formation establishments.

Cummings notes that there is little said of marriage and the diaconate in the *Dogmatic Constitution on the Church* (*Lumen Gentium* 29). In fact, against the background of the conciliar debates about the risk to priestly celibacy, it could be argued that there was in this constitution little more than a grudging acceptance that married men might become deacons. Cummings speaks of an "undeveloped and underdeveloped theology of marriage" in relation to the diaconate but takes the view that perhaps "the experience of marriage is the ingredient for such a development to occur."[7] In a chapter entitled "Diaconal Marriage" in *Deacons and the Church*, Cummings makes a strong statement about the significance of marriage in diaconal ministry. In even choosing the term "diaconal marriage" rather than simply "married deacons", the emphasis shifts from the deacon's family being a form of collateral damage, which must be accepted as part of his ministry, to being a vital and enriching aspect of his ministerial life. Cummings sketches the parallels between the rites of marriage and ordination – the public celebration of the rites and the setting of both sacraments in the context of Baptism and the power of the Holy Spirit. Matrimony is described as a sacrament of enrichment and strengthening whilst the prayer of diaconal consecration speaks of the strengthening of the deacon to serve the local Church faithfully in self-gift. Cummings, however, senses that the Sacrament of Marriage is somehow not given equal status when set beside Holy Orders. He notes:

> Central to the Sacrament of Marriage is the right ordering of sexuality, one of the most powerful of human forces and dynamics. Yet there is a general reluctance to acknowledge the experience of sexuality as God-given and as a mediating encounter with God.[8]

Cummings cites Rahner's call to awareness of the true theology of marriage:

> It must always be borne in mind ... that in a true theology of marriage, marriage must really and truly not be regarded as a mere concession to human weakness... but must be seen to have an absolutely positive and essential function, not only in the private Christian life

of certain individuals but also in the Church. Marriage, understood as a sacramentally consecrated union, is both in and for the Church the concrete and real representation and living example of the mystery of Christ's union with the Church.[9]

This affirmation that "human sexuality is of God and is not without the presence of God[10] is perhaps a healthy starting point for the formulation of a theology of diaconal marriage.

The human ecology model of the diaconate – a social scientific approach

Like his critique of diaconal marriage, the concept of the diaconal "ecosystem" is derived from Latcovich's project with deacons and their spouses in the Diocese of Cleveland, Ohio in 1994. This concept draws upon the work of eminent sociologists Ralph Turner and Herbert Blumer. Whilst it is not my intention to stray from a theological path, it is nonetheless appropriate to put social scientific and anthropological method into the service of theology. Furthermore, it seems relevant to situate the presenting issues into the wider context of society at large since this is where the lives of deacons are lived out and from where much of our understanding is derived. In the three-way reflective conversation alluded to at the beginning of the chapter, the human ecology model of diaconate can be seen to represent "prevailing culture" and articulate some of the difficulties which Church communities and wider society may have in understanding what the ministry of permanent deacons is about.

At its simplest, the model is depicted as a Venn diagram which illustrates three "environments" for the deacon's family as compared with two which are common to most families. Circle A represents the secular role or careers of both the deacon and his wife. Circle B is described as "the microsystem of family relations where the deacon and his wife are spouses and parents." These two environments are common to most families in today's society and are known to impact on one another. Circle C represents the environment of diaconal ministry which completes the "ecosystem", and it is the interplay between the ministerial microsystem and its

Baptising Babies and Clearing Gutters

relationship to the other microsystems which provided the focus of Latcovich's 1994 study. (Note: The label "family" has been added to the marriage microsystem as this is clearly implied in Latcovich's account, but not explicitly depicted in his original diagram. "Secular job" has also been altered to "secular role/profession" as this more accurately reflects a British mode of expression.) Latcovich found that the ministerial demands on the deacon's time provided "high level stimulation" in contrast to some of the other activities which the deacon was obliged to undertake. Preaching at two Masses, preparing a couple for marriage, baptising a child, demanded the greatest use of his abilities and that, in contrast, he might receive "contrary and ambiguous signals from his job or family if the ministerial demands outweigh the others."[11] This has certainly been the experience of many of the Southwark Province deacons, who have expressed regret at their lack of time with both spouses and families.

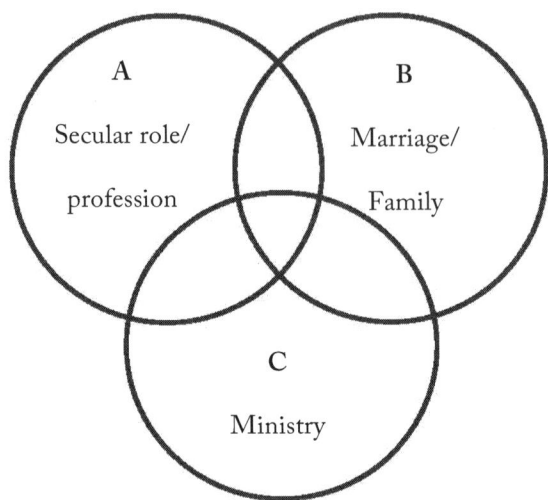

Latcovich's Human Ecology Model of the Permanent Diaconate

Latcovich goes on to explore the "role-taking" which the deacon is required to embrace as part of Holy Orders and sets this in the context of the work of sociologist Herbert Blumer, who held that society can be conceived as an exchange of gestures which involves the use of symbols for communicating and defining roles.¹² In the context of the permanent diaconate, Latcovich takes the view that when a married man is ordained a deacon, he and his wife find themselves "being a clergyman and the wife of a clergyman" in accordance with a set of accepted symbols and gestures:

> The clergyman's role in Roman Catholicism has been defined from a long-standing cultural and social structure and the cultural norm, stereotypes and 'social cues' of this role have created a set of conditions for the one who 'plays' that role. For example a clergyman is expected to wear clerical garb and liturgical vestments, to pray the Office of the Church, to function in various ministries of service, to act in a dignified and proper manner by distinguishing himself from the secular world and to live a celibate lifestyle. While a deacon is no longer required to be celibate (he may be married), his lifestyle in many ways is culturally viewed much like the normative view of the Catholic priest.¹³

The Southwark Province deacons have testified to their experiences of role-taking in response to the "social cues" given by their parishioners. The deacons of the 1970s cohort experienced the dismay of their communities who felt that only celibate ministers should touch sacred vessels and be present within the confines of the sanctuary. This adverse "social cue" has now been replaced by an easy acceptance, not only of the deacon's place at the altar, but the lay reader's contribution at the ambo and the Extraordinary Minister of Holy Communion's role in the liturgical and pastoral life of the parish.

The tendency of colleagues in the workplace to expect a stereotypical deacon to display a pious clerical persona has now been balanced by those who have shown affirming support and guided colleagues in difficulties to seek out "our" deacon for pastoral guidance.

The pressures experienced by the deacon's children to observe a higher standard of good conduct have been noted as unhelpful "exemplarism." Again, this view is balanced by an acceptance by some family members that "Dad has always been involved in Church."

Since there is no recent tradition of Roman Catholic priest's spouse, the cultural norm for the vicar's wife appears to have been applied by many parishioners and those in the wider community. For some, this is a role of "first responder" when parishioners wish to contact the deacon, whilst for others there is a "joint ministry" approach which can itself prove problematic for those who see the diaconal ministry as strictly reserved to the one who has been ordained. It is also important to acknowledge that the cultural norms for the vicar's wife may themselves have changed in recent years as many clergymen's wives now undertake careers in their own right, not least because of the financial imperative to sustain a reasonable standard of living. Roman Catholic parish communities should therefore exercise caution in applying outmoded cultural norms for the deacon's spouse in terms of pastoral ministry. Similarly, deacons and their spouses should be mindful not to model norms which are unrealistic for their pastoral situation.

Latcovich provides a diagrammatic representation of the "symbolic interactionist" perspective of the deacon's role.

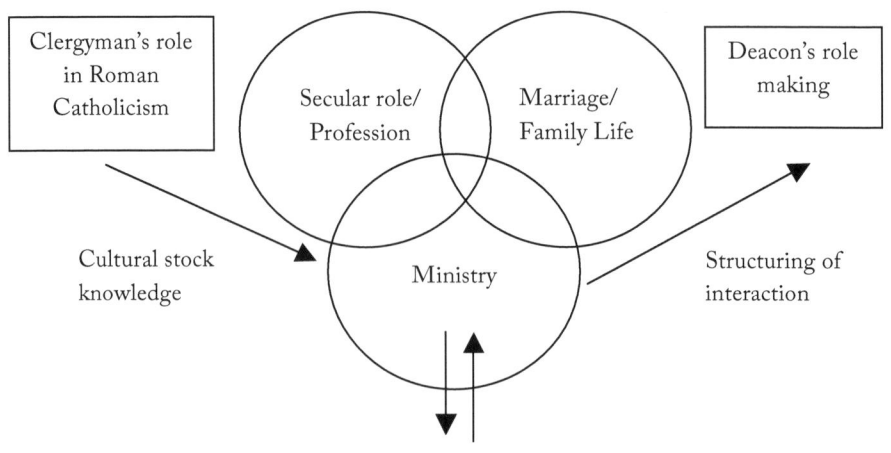

Latcovich's Diaconal Role Taking

| Inviting Theological Conversations

As the diagram illustrates, the role of the deacon reflects many past cultural and symbolic social cues which were reserved for celibate priests in the Church. However, as Latcovich notes, "the 'actor' in this case, needs to communicate and use symbols that represent his situation. Therefore as the model suggests, the interaction of the diaconate ecosystem must validate the preconceived role. The dual direction of the arrows in the figure suggests that the deacon must give a new interpretation or "definition" of his situation. He presents himself through an interpretation of his roles as a layperson (husband, father and employee) and as an ordained minister (dressing sometimes in clerical garb, performing liturgical, pastoral and sacramental roles). It is necessary for his spouse to define her situation as "the spouse of a Roman Catholic deacon". The deacon must utilise the existing stock knowledge of "what a clergyman is" but define his own situation from his environment. Latcovich argues that:

> ...the deacon's own symbolic actions will give meaning to the role he is required to embrace and this will require him to interpret his family life, job and ministry by creating a meaningful and integrated lifestyle within the existing structures. While the Church as a social structure has created a hierarchical role for the deacon as an ordained minister, the authentic role of the married deacon must be achieved through his own basic direction and orientation within the social structure of the Church. Church structures relegate specific functions to the office of deacon. However, the diaconate as a collective unit must choose the symbols that interpret the three microsystems of their environment i.e. family, professional role and ministry".[14]

For personal reflection or for discussion in small groups

1. Which symbols/emblems do you think best represent the ministry of the deacon?
2. What symbols/emblems if any are unhelpful in depicting the deacon's role?

Endnotes

---

[1] Latcovich, M. 1996. *The Effects of the Ministerial Environment on RC Permanent Deacons and their Spouses*. Case Western University

[2] Ibid piii

[3] Rahner, K. 1963. *The Church and the Sacraments*. Freiburg:Herder and Herder. p.107 cited by Latcovich in "The Diaconate and Marriage: A Sociological Reflection" in Keating, J. (ed) 2003. *The Deacon Reader*. New York: Paulist Press. p. 223.

[4] Kasper, W. 1980. *Theology of Marriage*. New York: Crossroad. p.38 cited by Latcovich in "The Diaconate and Marriage: A Sociological Reflection" in Keating, J. (ed) 2003. *The Deacon Reader*. New York: Paulist Press. p. 223.

[5] Ibid p.224.

[6] Meehan writing in Chapter 13 of *The Deacon Reader* states that since its inception of the diaconate formation programme, wives have always been invited to attend. In the late 1970s, they were "encouraged" to attend and by the mid 1980s, they were "strongly encouraged". This was perceived as an expectation to attend and by 2004, this has become full participation in the programme although no official church requirement has changed (Footnote p232).

[7] Cummings, O.F. 2004. *Deacons and the Church*. New York: Paulist Press.p.94.

[8] Ibid p.100.

[9] Rahner, K. 1993. "The Theology of the Restoration of the Diaconate" in *Foundations for the Renewal of the Diaconate*. Washington DC: United States Conference of Catholic Bishops 1993: p. 163 cited by Cummings, O.F. 2004. *Deacons and the Church*. New York: Paulist Press. p. 101.

[10] Cummings, O.F. 2004. *Deacons and the Church*. New York: Paulist Press. p. 101.

[11] Latcovich, M. 1996. *The Effects of the Ministerial Environment on RC Permanent Deacons and their Spouses*. Case Western University. p.16.

[12] Blumer, H. 1969. *Symbolic Interactionism: Perspective and Method*. New Jersey: Prentice-Hall Press p87-88 cited by Latcovich M in *The Effects of the Ministerial Environment on RC Permanent Deacons and their Spouses*. Case Western University. p.16.

[13] Latcovich 1996 p:27

[14] Ibid p.29

10 | Exploring the Diaconal "Microsystems"

Using Latcovich's diaconal ecosystem model, the empirical data from the deacons of Southwark Province can be presented as a set of creative tensions, reflecting both the negative and positive experiences of the respondents. The Venn Diagram of the deacon's family, professional and ministerial lives can be disassembled into its component parts and the research findings summarised under three headings.

The deacon's professional life

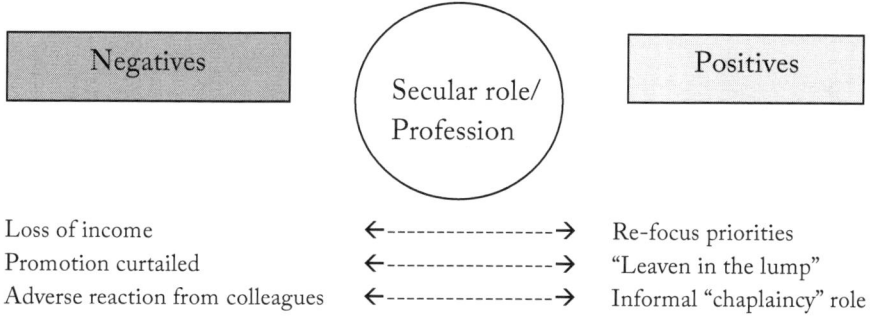

Creative tensions within the deacon's professional "microsystem"

The above figure reflects the deacons' responses to those questions relating to the impact of their ministry on their professional lives. The loss of income and curtailment of promotion relate to the commitment of the deacons to their ministerial role over and against the needs of their profession or employer. The adverse reactions from colleagues have resulted from either anti-religious attitudes or the presumption that the deacon will perhaps be countercultural in the workplace. As noted earlier, one respondent mentioned that there was concern in the senior ranks of management because they did not want a "holy Joe approach to business matters". Another mentioned that the adverse reaction to his ministry came from Roman Catholic colleagues. These negative experiences are balanced by a preference for diaconal ministry through a change in priorities, a recognition that he can be a willing "leaven in the lump" or, indeed, given recognition in the workplace as a man in Holy Orders who can be entrusted with problems and confidences. Some respondents had been approached by colleagues for guidance and support and some had conducted funeral services for colleagues and their families.

The deacon's marriage and family life

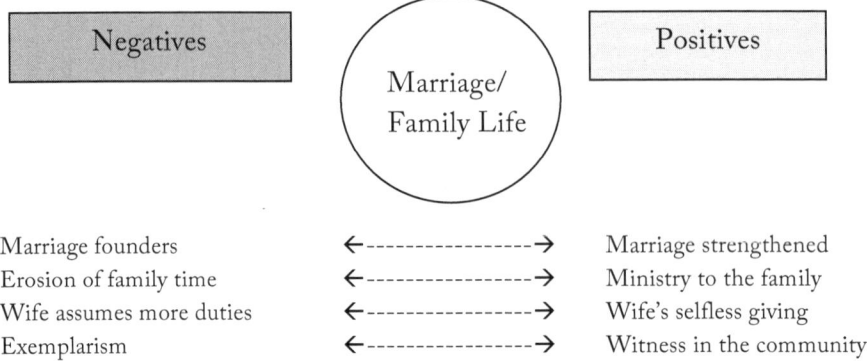

Creative tensions within the deacon's marital and family "microsystem"

As the figure indicates, the negative end of the spectrum of family and married life for the deacon is characterised by irreparable damage to the marriage, erosion of time made available for spouse and family, the relegation of more duties to the wife than appear reasonable, and the strain upon the deacon's children, and indeed his wife, to lead exemplary lives in the public gaze of the parish and wider community. Fortunately, the Southwark respondents had a low incidence of marriage failure but there were significant pressures around the management of time available for a fulfilling family-oriented lifestyle. Wives frequently found themselves in the role of "first responder", welcoming visitors connected to their husbands' ministry into their homes.

At the positive end of the spectrum was the acknowledged enrichment of the marriage through a shared prayer life and shared ministry, although in many cases, the deacon's wife had previously undertaken pastoral ministry in her own right rather than in the context of her husband's diaconal calling. Ministry to the family provided a counterbalance to the acknowledged erosion of family time, some deacons having baptised their grandchildren, officiated at the weddings of family members and at the funeral rites of parents or friends. The sacrificial self-giving of deacons' wives was acknowledged by many respondents and balances the negative reactions of wives feeling overburdened with family and other duties. Finally, the powerful public witness of the deacon's family life was felt by many respondents to be a sign of their own accessibility to others and empathy for the strains and stresses which routinely occur in modern family life.

The deacon's ministerial life

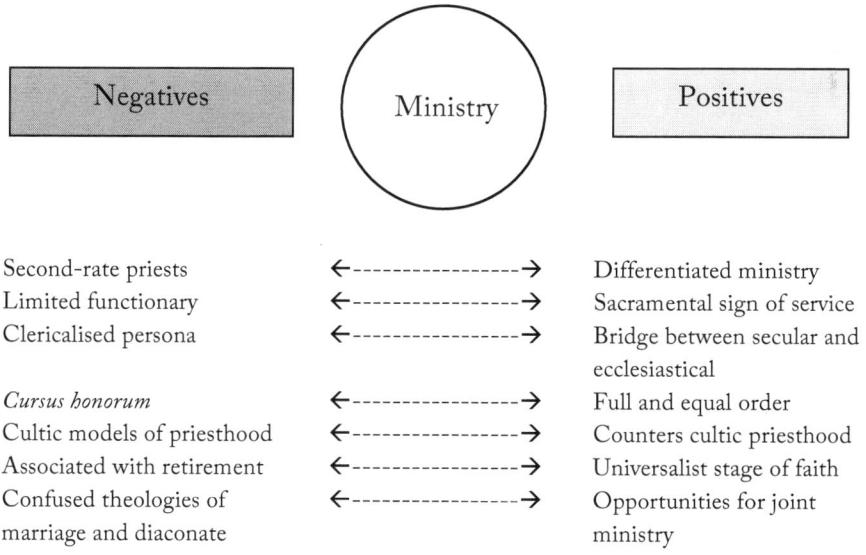

Negatives		Positives
Second-rate priests	←----------------→	Differentiated ministry
Limited functionary	←----------------→	Sacramental sign of service
Clericalised persona	←----------------→	Bridge between secular and ecclesiastical
Cursus honorum	←----------------→	Full and equal order
Cultic models of priesthood	←----------------→	Counters cultic priesthood
Associated with retirement	←----------------→	Universalist stage of faith
Confused theologies of marriage and diaconate	←----------------→	Opportunities for joint ministry

Creative tensions within the deacon's ministerial "microsystem"

The figure illustrates the range of tensions which prevail in the deacon's ministerial ecosystem. Many of these are the direct consequence of a limited understanding of the theology of the diaconate. For example, the notion that the deacon is a "second-rate priest" or a limited functionary casts him solely in a liturgical role which inevitably finds him wanting, as he is not permitted to preside at the Eucharist or to administer the Sacrament of Reconciliation or Sacrament of the Sick. One of the project's interviewees, involved in clerical formation in a seminary alluded to this difficulty:

> People's understanding is quite sketchy or difficult... I think as a concept in itself, the diaconate is not really adequately understood. Generally, people don't really distinguish the difference between what the priest is and does and what the deacon is and does. They might see some practical consequences but you'd frequently hear people where they are not used to seeing deacons saying "Do you do Mass?" or asking questions about what they are capable of or what their function is. I suppose in parishes where you've got a permanent deacon and people see what activities he does and what activities he doesn't do they can probably start to distinguish more but I think that for most people there is probably just a "clerical lump" and that divides into some different jobs. So I think to try and engage with where people are, to try and spell out what deacons are, what they do, is quite difficult. And I think that is probably an inheritance from our long and insistent focus on the priesthood – even only by Vatican II are we starting to get a balance and start talking about bishops and since then we now have got the diaconate to deal with...when people's primary and central focus is the priest and the celebration of the Mass or what their experience of parish is. So I suppose, timewise, we are only just opening these out.

Clericalised persona

In terms of the "clericalised persona" of the deacon, the wearing of clerical garb has been identified as problematical for some. Different approaches apply in different dioceses, with some bishops discouraging their deacons from wearing clerical garb except on formal occasions. In Southwark Archdiocese for example, "it is considered appropriate that the deacon should wear clerical dress when exercising his ministry in a public way."[1] However it could be argued that the deacon, when undertaking charitable works is indeed exercising his ministry in a public way but that clerical garb might be entirely inappropriate. Also, some deacons have opted to wear a form of clerical garb which is normally associated with the priesthood i.e. black suit, black shirt and Roman collar. This can cause some confusion and disquiet. In terms of "symbolic interactionism" there is perhaps an opportunity for deacons to reinterpret the norms of clerical garb in order to better differentiate their ministry from priesthood e.g. the adoption of the deacon's pin on a lapel or the wearing of a Roman collar in a shirt which is not black. This is particularly important in healthcare settings where people being ministered to may be frail or confused. It should, however, be acknowledged that the sign value of the Roman collar lends authority to the deacon's ministry, giving affirmation of his pastoral credentials to those to whom he is ministering. This relates again to the stock knowledge of our understanding of what it means to be a man in Roman Catholic Holy Orders.

The *Cursus Honorum* and a full and equal order

The *Cursus Honorum* is the term used to differentiate the three ranks of Holy Orders, of which the diaconate is the lowest, followed by the presbyterate and the episcopate, which is the "fullness of order."[2] As has been noted in the analysis of the deacon's questionnaires, diaconal leadership if perceived only in a hierarchical progression will always be seen to fall short of the leadership of the priest. The *cursus honorum* is regarded by Ditewig as a major challenge to the contemporary diaconate and calls for fresh thinking about the sacramental nature of the Church and its ordering of ministry. He urges an "organic approach to ministry", seeing the diaconate as related to but independent of the presbyterate, noting that when the Church operated under a priest-centred model of ordained ministry all other orders were seen in relation to eventual ordination to the presbyterate. Ditewig feels that it is both unnecessary and undesirable to continue to ordain seminarians as deacons as part of their formation for the priesthood.³ He points to other vestiges of the *cursus honorum* – the ordination of bishops from the order of presbyters and the installation of candidates for the priesthood and the diaconate into the ministries of lector and acolyte. Although these ministries were adapted from the minor orders by Pope Paul VI,⁴ their roots are in the suppressed minor orders. This subtly reinforces the *cursus honorum* even though it was supposedly abandoned at Vatican II. Ditewig takes the view that there is no doctrinal necessity for one order to lead inexorably to the next. He states:

> The bishop is now regarded as the prime minister, with two derivative orders, presbyters and deacons who assist him in sacerdotal and diaconal ways. In short, rather than an ascending progression that makes a 'higher' order dependent upon receiving a 'lesser' order, it is the other way round: the bishop with the fullness of orders is responsible for sharing his ministry with two assisting orders.⁵

The deacon and cultic models of priesthood

In the 2005 paper *On the Way to Life – A Study by The Heythrop Institute for Religion, Ethics and Public Life*, Hanvey draws attention to a possible dissonance in priestly ministry between two groups of priests – those who favour a "Servant Model" of priesthood and those who tend towards a "Cultic Model". Alluding to the research of Hoge and Wenger in the USA, Hanvey highlights the shift from 'the servant-leader model' (SM) prevalent after the Second Vatican Council to a 'cultic model' (CM) a trend which seems to become noticeable in the 1980s:

> The characteristics are significant not only for relationships between older and younger generations of

clergy but for relationships to laity as well. While recognising the dangers in stereotyping, Hoge and Wenger do detect significant contrasting patterns. For the SM group, the priest is a pastoral leader; for CM 'a man set apart'. Regarding attitudes to authority, SM displayed a 'values flexibility' whereas CM shows a 'values strict hierarchy'. In terms of liturgy, one group allowed for creativity, the other followed the rules. In terms of theology, CM tended to defend 'orthodoxy' while the other allowed for theological difference. For SM, celibacy was seen as optional for priesthood, while CM saw it as essential. Strong judgmental attitudes were also noted: the young CM priests thought of the older ones as 'a lost generation', secularised and anti-establishment. The younger CM priests thought of themselves as traditional, conservative, 'unapologetically Catholic' and ecclesiologically sound. Of course, the differences were not as strongly polarised in practice: …all agreed on the love for God's people, desire to serve God's people, love for the Catholic Church, desire for personal fulfilment and acceptance of celibate homosexual priests…. The polarization today concerns ecclesiology, the theology of priesthood, and the liturgy.[6]

Hanvey does not indicate how this creative tension will play out in the ministry of the diaconate, but it is clear that it will inevitably have an impact. Interviewee A felt that the deacon might provide a helpful counterbalance to the cultic model, being the one who affects constant movement between the priest and the people throughout the liturgy.[7]

A further development in liturgical practice (although some might describe it as regression) was heralded by Pope Benedict XVI's Apostolic Letter *Summorum Pontificum on the use of the Roman Liturgy prior to the Reform of 1970*, given on 7 July 2007. In his letter, Pope Benedict VI affirmed the use of the pre-Vatican II Latin Rite Mass. His letter states:

The last version of the *Missale Romanum* prior to the Council, which was published with the authority of Pope John XXIII in 1962 and used during the Council, will now be able to be used as a *Forma Extraordinaria* of the liturgical celebration. It is not appropriate to speak of these two versions of the Roman Missal as if they were 'two Rites'. Rather, it is a matter of a twofold use of one and the same rite.[8]

Although this reaffirmation of the Extraordinary Form was intended to be a gesture of fraternal regard for Lefebvrist bishops who had been excommunicated because of their rejection of the liturgical changes of the Second Vatican Council, the initiative has perhaps awakened anxiety of a return to a more cultic form of priesthood which emphasises the secular/sacred divide. It is difficult to situate the permanent deacon liturgically within the Extraordinary Rite since his role in the Ordinary Rite affects movement between the sanctuary and nave. In the Extraordinary Rite, the liturgical emphasis is placed within the sanctuary in a rite which excludes the active involvement of lay people.

Only in the proclamation of the Gospel in the Tridentine High Mass is the deacon's task similar to that of the permanent deacon in the Ordinary Rite of the New Order i.e. having brought the book of the Gospels to the priest, he asks for a blessing before solemnly bearing the book to the ambo. In this case however, he chants the gospel, after which, the subdeacon takes the open book to the priest and offers it to him to kiss. In the Extraordinary Form, the gifts are not brought to the altar from the nave and there is no reception of the gifts since the bread and wine are already within the sanctuary. The deacon's next active involvement in the Extraordinary Form rite is the incensing of the celebrant, followed by the other ranks of clergy and finally the faithful "in token of their offering of themselves with the Divine Victim of the Mass".[9] The next rubric for the Tridentine Rite deacon is to receive the kiss of peace, "who gives it to the Subdeacon, who in turn gives it to the clergy present. Although this gesture symbolises "the love which should unite all Christians who are one Body in Christ," the congregation is not actively involved in this symbolic gesture. The High Mass dismissal is sung by the deacon, after which the priest says the final prayer and gives the people his blessing.

Clearly the rubrics which are given for deacons (and subdeacons) in the 1963 Missal are directed either at those seminarians who have not yet been ordained to the priesthood or to priests who are performing the roles of deacons and subdeacons. This rite does not reflect the liturgical ministry of the contemporary permanent deacon, whose role is clearly elaborated in the *General Instruction of the Roman Missal (GIRM)* as one who "has his own part in proclaiming the Gospel, in preaching God's word from time to time, in announcing the intentions of the Prayer of the Faithful, in ministering to the priest, in preparing the altar and serving the celebration of the Sacrifice, in distributing the Eucharist to the faithful, especially under the species of wine and sometimes in giving directions regarding the people's gestures and posture".[10] In the Low Mass of the Extraordinary Form, the deacon is not present in the sanctuary at all and his roles in High Mass reflect the *Cursus Honorum* and not "a full and equal order" with its own threefold ministry.

Diaconate as a role for the retired or a feature of a "universalist"[11] stage of faith

The creative tension identified here is the association of the permanent diaconate with retirement and that it is perhaps a form of pastoral "hobby" for those who no longer work in full-time careers or indeed, a form of recognition for years of faithful service in the parish. This perception is due in part to the requirements for deacons to be men of mature age i.e. over thirty-five years old and financially independent. The 53 Southwark Province respondents to the research questionnaire were aged 41 – 88 years (average 64, median 62). The respondents in the Ushaw research of 2007 yielded a similar age profile. The association of the diaconate with retirement age is perhaps unhelpful if the nature of the diaconal ministry is fundamentally one of active service, including the workplace and civic life. As was noted earlier, the range of charitable endeavours and virtuous work carried out by deacons is considerable, with many engaged in active voluntary service as private individuals and as representatives of the local Catholic community in inter-denominational and interfaith groups.

It should be remembered that, of the three ranks of Holy Orders, only deacons are permitted to hold roles in political and public life.[12] Unlike their brothers in the presbyterate and episcopate, they may participate in the exercise of civil power and in all aspects of appropriate trade and commerce. They do, however, require the permission of the bishop in order to do so. In this way, they can respond to the challenges of *Gaudium et Spes* both in their personal lives and as the public witness to the work of the Church:

> Christians engaged actively in modern economic and social progress and in the struggle for justice and charity must be convinced that they have much to contribute to the prosperity of humanity and to world peace. Let them as individuals and as a group, give a shining example to others. Endowed with the skill and experience so absolutely necessary for them, let them preserve a proper sense of values in their earthly activity in loyalty to Christ and his gospel.[13]

Confused theologies of marriage and diaconate

Consideration has already been given to the theology of marriage in the context of the permanent diaconate in the section entitled "Deacon's Marriage/Family Microsystem". However one final observation is worthy of inclusion. In the contemporary Church, the discipline of celibacy, which must be observed by deacons whose wives pre-decease them, may signal an underlying disapproval of marriage for those in Holy Orders. Whilst it is acceptable for married men to become deacons, unmarried deacons must remain celibate and deacons who become widowers must also eschew the future comfort and companionship of further marriage.[14] The prohibition on digamy for clergy (remarriage after the death of the first spouse) has its roots in the early Church. For example, 1 Timothy 3.12 refers to the requirement for deacons to be married only once. Similarly in the letter to Titus 1:6, the elders must be of "irreproachable character" and "married only once". In the Patristic era, the writings of both Tertullian and Origen insist that monogamy is observed and in the case of Origen, he distinguishes:

> ...the monogamous, the virgin, the perpetually chaste, to belong to the Church of God; while the digamist, however moral his behaviour, however strong in virtues he may be is yet not of the Church of God...but of the second grade, of those who call on the name of the Lord.[15]

As was noted in Chapter 2, the Church Councils of Arles, and Elvira urged clergy to desist from sexual relations with their wives.

In his account of "Priestly celibacy in Patristics and in the History of the Church",[16] Roman Cholij, the secretary of the Apostolic Exarch for Ukranian Catholics in Great Britain admits that:

> It is true that, in the patristic age, the marked sense of the transcendence of God led to an anthropology that relativized many of the values of marriage to the things of this world. Relative to the things of God, sexual activity could be described in terms that draw on the vocabulary of Levitical ritualism but which offend the linguistic sensibilities of our own time.

Although an appeal to history may be seen to justify this discipline of sexual abstinence, it nonetheless appears to point to a systemic disapproval of conjugal love and militates against the view of theologians like Rahner and Kasper who uphold marriage and its sexuality as being holy and of God.

In terms of the canonical imposition[17] on the deacon to remain celibate after the decease of his wife, there are limited exceptions: if the deacon's children are of tender age when their mother dies or if he has elderly parents or parents-in-law who require care, or if his service is of "great and proven usefulness" to the work of the diocese, then a dispensation for remarriage may be sought.[18] However, as one interviewee expressed it:

> ...it does suggest a fairly stereotypical view of the wife's role but that opens up a new avenue of research...You

would have to argue on the basis of 'I am doing this for my kids' benefit' – the fact that I love this woman and feel called to a relationship with her is kind of…..they don't want sex to rear its ugly head.

In the context of a theological conversation between the Church's tradition and teaching and prevailing culture, the discipline of clerical celibacy for widower deacons appears somewhat problematical.

For personal reflection or for discussion in small groups

1. What safeguards should be put in place in order to ensure that the deacon is able to achieve a healthy work/life/ministry balance?
2. Explore how the equality of the sacraments of marriage and Holy Orders can be lived out in the parish.
3. What are your views about the prohibition of remarriage for widower deacons?

Endnotes

---

[1] *The Permanent Diaconate in the Diocese of Southwark* 1994 p 11. Some American dioceses e.g. Austin Texas insist that clerical dress is reserved only for specific settings i.e. prison ministry and only with specific written approval of the bishop.

[2] *Dogmatic Constitution on the Church (Lumen Gentium)* 1964 in Flannery, A. (ed) 1996 *Vatican Council II – Constitutions, Decrees, Declarations.* New York: Costello. LG41

[3] Interviewee B echoes this view. "While we still have this halfway system, I think we do not do justice to the theology of vocation. It is strange theologically to ordain someone to a ministry to which they have never felt called. It does a disservice to a fundamental understanding of what we mean by vocation".

[4] Paul VI. 1972. *Ministeria Quaedam* 1972 " Among the particular offices to be preserved and adapted to contemporary needs are those that are in a special way more closely connected with the ministries of the word and of the altar and that in the Latin Church are called the offices of *reader* and

acolyte and the subdiaconate. It is fitting to preserve and adapt these in such a way, that from this time on there will be two offices: that of reader and that of acolyte, which will include the functions of the subdiaconate". *Ministeria Quaedam* 4.

[5] Ditewig, W.T. 2007. *The Emerging Diaconate*. New York: Paulist Press. pp.207-208.

[6] Hanvey, J. and T. Carroll. 2005. *On the Way to Life*. http://beta.rcdow.org.uk/att/files/faith/aff/on+the+way+to+life.pdf accessed 25/10/2012

[7] Interviewee A 25 September 2008 expressed it as follows: "There is so much movement of them (deacons) between the people and the sanctuary or the altar ...particularly identified with taking out what has been confected ...the distribution of communion, drawing people in at the gifts so that sense of the sanctuary as a private domain – in some ways the role of the deacon is to militate against that all the time ...if we are seeing the priest as more static in the celebration of the rite then the deacon is constantly moving from the priest ...being commissioned to go down and proclaim the gospel and often going out to do the things that the deacon is concerned with in the celebration of the Eucharist are always affecting connections"

[8] Benedict XVI 2007. *Summorum Pontificum*. http://www.vatican.va/holy_father/benedict_xvi/letters/2007/documents/hf_benxvi_let_20070707_lettera-vescovi_en.html accessed 25/10/2012 – Libreria Editrice Vaticana (© Libreria Editrice Vaticana, 2013).

[9] Rubric of the Roman Missal 1963

[10] Catholic Bishops Conference of England and Wales 2005. *General Instruction of the Roman Missal*. London:Catholic Truth Society. GIRM 94

[11] This stage of faith has been identified by James Fowler as one which is achieved in maturity by those who live their lives fully in the service of others. Fowler's seven stages of faith are summarised at: http://faculty.plts.edu/gpence/ html/fowler.htm accessed 26/06/2013.

[12] Can. 288 The prescripts of cann. 284, 285, §§3 and 4, 286, and 287, §2 do not bind permanent deacons unless particular law establishes otherwise. http://www.vatican.va/archive/ENG1104/__PY.HTM – Libreria Editrice Vaticana (© Libreria Editrice Vaticana, 2013).
accessed 25/10/2012

[13] *Pastoral Constitution on the Church in the Modern World. (Gaudium et Spes)*. 1965 in Flannery, A. (ed) 1996 *Vatican Council II – Constitutions, Decrees, Declarations*. New York: Costello. GS72.

[14] In similar vein, married clergy from other denominations who seek to be

ordained as Roman Catholic priests are required to sign a declaration that they will not seek remarriage in the event of their spouse's death and " accept the Bishop's Conference reaffirmation of its commitment to the law of celibacy" (Portsmouth Diocese's Application for Ordination to the Catholic Priesthood).

[15] "*Homily In Lucam xvii*" in Bettenson, H. (ed) 1963. *The Early Christian Fathers – A Selection from the Writings of the Fathers from St Clement of Rome to Athanasius.* Translated by H. Bettenson:. Oxford: Oxford University Press. p.351.

[16] Cholij,R. "Priestly celibacy in Patristics and in the History of the Church" http://www.vatican.va/roman_curia/congregations/cclergy/documents/rc_con_cclergy_doc_01011993_chisto_en.html accessed 06/09/2010 – Libreria Editrice Vaticana (© Libreria Editrice Vaticana, 2013).

[17] Canon 1087 states that "Those in sacred orders invalidly attempt marriage."

[18] The Congregation for Divine Worship and the Discipline of the Sacraments letter of 6 June 1997 refers to the modification of the norm which had required three cumulative and simultaneous conditions for the granting of the dispensation, "hence any one of the three conditions, taken singly" would suffice. See Beal et al *New Commentary on the Code of Canon Law.* New York: Paulist Press. pp.358-359).

11 | Diaconal Formation to Support the People of God

This chapter explores what model of formation best suits the contemporary permanent deacon to serve the people of God. Traditionally, the formation of Roman Catholic clergy has taken place in seminaries, with the aspirants "set apart" from their communities and families. For permanent deacons with "day jobs" and family life, this model of preparation is inappropriate. Instead, their formation is undertaken in weekend sessions held within seminary premises (as in St John's Seminary, Wonersh) but without contact with the resident student body of seminarians. This has certain disadvantages in so far as the priestly aspirants and their diaconal counterparts do not get the opportunity to discuss their respective charisms until they work together in parish placements.

In this chapter, I will explore the formation framework offered by Pope John Paul II's post-synodal exhortation given on 25 March 1992, *Pastores Dabo Vobis (PDV)*[1] Although this document was directed "To the Bishops, Clergy and Faithful on the Formation of Priests in the Circumstances of the Present Day", it has much to offer the permanent deacon. Reflecting the expressed theology of Vatican II, any analysis of either priest or deacon benefits from a starting pointing in the episcopate, "the fullness of order". The roles of both priests and deacons can arguably only be fully understood in the context of the episcopate. As Interviewee A notes:

> I would want to begin from a sense of there being one Sacrament of Order which is expressed in three modes and so that priests don't stop expressing diaconate, or shouldn't, and bishops certainly shouldn't… there is a cumulative sense that comes through with Vatican II specifically talking about the bishops expressing the

'fullness of order' ... the important thing is to move back from that fullness and ...where there would be a unique position for what we call permanent deacons would be that they permanently express that element which is one part of the whole, whereas priests and bishops express that as part of a continuum.

Seen in this light, the formation of deacons and priests should be perceived as an integrated whole. Interviewee A recalled that as soon as Bishop Worlock introduced the permanent diaconate in the Archdiocese of Liverpool, all deacons, both permanent and transitional, were ordained together in the cathedral. He added:

...I think obviously to show that these are not actually two different ministries, that although one is going on to take on a different role, that, at this point there is a commonality between them. I think that, as a symbol, that did work well, but I think it would work better if there was more connection in the training.

In Section 2 of the Introduction to PDV, the following could stand as a vision statement for all in Holy Orders, but for this exercise, "permanent deacon" will be substituted for "priest".

The formation of future deacons, both diocesan and religious, and lifelong assiduous care for their personal sanctification in the ministry and for the constant updating of their pastoral commitment is considered by the Church one of the most demanding and important tasks for the future of the evangelisation of humanity.

The apostolic exhortation sets ministerial priesthood, and by implication, the diaconate, "within the Church's mystery, as a mystery of Trinitarian communion in missionary tension". In PDV16 the explicit relationship to the bishop is articulated... "through the priesthood of the bishop, the priesthood of the second order is incorporated in the apostolic structure of the Church". Similarly, the priesthood of the third order i.e. the diaconate, is also incorporated in the apostolic structure of the Church and, like priests, they can be seen to be called:

> ...to serve the faith, hope and charity of the laity. They recognise and uphold, as brothers and friends the dignity of the laity as children of God and help them to exercise fully their specific role in the overall context of the Church's mission (PDV17).

In PDV 26, which highlights the threefold ministry of the priest to word, sacrament and pastoral charity, there is much to anchor the deacon's ministry. The sacred minister is called to foster a personal familiarity with the word of God, not only in its interpretation and language but he must approach it with a "docile and prayerful heart so that it may penetrate his thoughts and feelings and bring about a new outlook in him, 'the mind of Christ' (1 Cor. 2:16)...he is not the master of the word but its servant."

The exhortation explores four areas of priestly formation – Human, Spiritual, Intellectual and Theological. A brief overview of each of the areas will serve to highlight the similarities and essential differences in the formation priorities of deacons and priests.

Human formation

Like their presbyteral fellow ministers, the deacon can rightly be urged to:

> ...mould his human personality in such a way that it becomes a bridge and not an obstacle for others in their meeting with Jesus Christ the Redeemer of humanity ... and... should be able to know the depths of the human heart, to perceive difficulties and problems, to make meeting and dialogue easy, to create trust and cooperation, to express serene and objective judgments (PDV 43).

The document then expounds the need to recognise the central role of love in life and the necessity in priestly formation for understanding the nuptuality of the body. This is, of course, set in the context of the discipline of priestly celibacy. However, if applied to the permanent diaconate, it can be developed to include a rich theology of diaconal marriage which has already been highlighted as a missing component in the deacon's formation.

Spiritual formation

PDV stresses that spiritual formation should be:

> ...conducted in such a way that the students may learn to live in intimate and unceasing union with God the Father through his Son, Jesus Christ, in the Holy Spirit....They should live (the) paschal Mystery in such a way that they will know how to initiate into it the people committed to their charge (PDV45).

Although deacons are not charged with the "cure of souls" in the manner of the priest or bishop, nonetheless, in their ministry to sacrament, word and charity they are equally called upon to become engaged in a lifelong friendship with Christ and a life-long search for God:

> So inexhaustible is the mystery of the imitation of Christ and the sharing in his life that this seeking will also have to continue throughout the priest's life and ministry (PDV46).

Likewise for the deacon. Spiritual formation also involves the seeking of Christ in people, and for this, the deacon is particularly well equipped as he is to be found in the workplace and the community in ways which priests are not. Mention has already been made of the fact that of the three priestly orders, only deacons may participate in public life. In this context, the deacon is particularly well placed to demonstrate preferential love for the poor and to do this officially in the name of the diocesan bishop and the local Church.

Intellectual formation

In this section, PDV finds the justification for intellectual formation in evangelisation. At a time when the Church is called upon to address issues of pluralism and engage meaningfully with scientific and technological discourse, sacred ministers must be equipped to proclaim the Gospel of Christ and to "make it credible to the legitimate demands of human reason" (PDV51). Although, clearly the theological and philosophical training of priests will, of necessity, be more rigorous, the intellectual formation of the permanent deacon is a vital component of his ongoing development. Although feedback from the Southwark Province deacons indicated that papal encyclicals and documents from the *Magisterium* are regarded as highly significant, there was little evidence of continuous facilitated learning opportunities for deacons in this regard. Their opportunities for evangelisation are more diverse than those of the presbyter, since the deacon may be witness in the workplace and in public life. Clearly, he must be able to articulate in a theologically creditable way the reason for his way of life.

Pastoral formation

The final pillar of PDV is the pastoral formation of priests, specifically pastoral or practical theology. As evidenced in the development of the foundation degree programme for Southwark Province diaconal students, the training of deacons is now underpinned by an academic accreditation, although their pastoral formation is carried out in the context of the communities in which they will minister. Unlike students for the priesthood who are formed in the "educational ecclesial community" of the seminary and undertake diaconal placements, the deacons' practical and pastoral skills are honed in the communities from which they have emerged and in which they will eventually serve. There is little evidence of the convergence of these two developmental streams, although deacons and priests are eventually called to minister together in parishes. In purely practical terms, the ability of diaconal students to meet with seminarians is severely curtailed by the needs of the former to be in their places of professional employment during the week and the needs of the latter to have rest and recreation at the weekend. However, in order to avoid the misunderstandings which have been demonstrated in this research about the role of the deacon in parish as a "filler of gaps" and "the bishop's man" etc. it would be beneficial to include within the core curriculum of Holy Orders formation appropriate modules which are undertaken jointly by priests and deacons.

The bishop as an agent of priestly formation

PDV highlights the presence of bishops as foundational to the formation of priests, not least because "it helps the seminary community live its insertion in the particular church and its communion with the pastor who guides it, but also because it verifies and encourages the pastoral purpose which is what specifies the entire formation of candidate for the priesthood" (PDV65). This episcopal connection is no less real for the deacon, who is the symbolic presence of the Church's ministry of charity, word and sacrament, carried out in direct response to his ministerial anointing by the bishop. For the deacon, the connection with the bishop provides "the *sensus ecclesiae* as a central spiritual and pastoral value" in the exercise of his ministry (PDV65).

The first generation of deacons testified to a close bond with their bishops whilst in formation, meeting with them regularly for tutorials and reflection. As the formation process became formalised and standardised, this close relationship has been lost. The theological connection between the deacon's ministry and that of the bishop is foundational to the deacon's self-understanding. It is recommended that opportunities are created for the deacons, as a diocesan entity, to meet regularly with their bishop so that the deacon's role as social intermediary is acknowledged and further developed.

Lay formation

Parish pastoral programmes do not currently provide high quality formation on the ministry of the deacon. Catholic Faith Exploration (CaFÉ) programmes, which are recommended by many diocesan formation departments, are impoverished in this respect. Even the National Vocations Office provides a somewhat perfunctory account of the deacon's role on its web site,[2] namely:

1. Visiting the sick and lonely, the bereaved, families and schools, taking communion to the housebound
2. Proclaiming the Gospel and preaching at Mass, teaching within the community and also celebrating the sacraments of baptism and marriage, taking funerals and leading public liturgies

The experience of respondents within Southwark Province has demonstrated that, whilst the communities have, in the main, welcomed their deacons, they may not be entirely sure of the significance of their presence among them. Some lay ministers have disapproved of the deacon, feeling that their own ministry has been threatened by his presence. At a time when lay ministry and the giftedness of all members of the people of God are beginning to be recognised and valued, the imposition of the "lower" ecclesiastical order to undertake activities like catechesis and Eucharistic ministry appears to some parishioners to be a retrograde step. However, properly understood in its theological context, the ministry of the deacon can be a stimulus for even greater lay involvement in the Church community.

There is a clear need for parish formation on the role of the deacon, particularly where his role is that of "ordinary " minister i.e. baptism and marriage and in other liturgies in which he may take the role of presider i.e. funeral services, liturgies of word and communion, and Benediction. It is also essential that his role in the Mass is properly understood. The symbolic significance of the deacon's presence within the Eucharistic assembly is not included in the major teaching documents on the Eucharist, published by the Catholic Bishops Conference of England and Wales. *One Bread One Body*, although published in 1998, remains a foundational document for formation in the theology of the Eucharist. However, this document does not expound the roles of the sacred ministers within the Eucharistic assembly. Similarly *With Hearts and Minds*, published in 2005, fails to explore the richness of the deacon's role. His task of inviting participation at the beginning of Mass and his ministry to the assembly in the proclamation of the word are not fully acknowledged. The Participant's Book of the resource refers to the ministry of the reader but does not distinguish the proclamation of the Gospel from the other readings. It refers to the possibility of a "reader" bearing the Book of the Gospels in the entrance procession and laying it upon the altar, and that the reader may also announce the intentions in the General Intercessions in the absence of a deacon.[3] The sacramental significance of these duties as part of the deacon's role in the Eucharist is not explained. One of his most significant contributions to the preparation of the gifts is the co-mingling of the water and wine and the recitation of the words "By the mystery of this water and wine may we come to share in the divinity of Christ, who humbled himself to share in our humanity."[4] In reciting this prayer, the deacon is granted the privilege of articulating the mystery of the Incarnation. However, it is not recited aloud and may go unnoticed by the assembly.

As the priest celebrant prays the concluding doxology for the Liturgy of the Eucharist, the deacon assists in holding the sacred species as the entire assembly proclaim the "Great Amen." In the Communion Rite, the deacon is the enabler and encourager of the people to offer each other the sign of peace – to be Christ to each other – and as the liturgy concludes, he enjoins them to go out to be Christ to the world. The deacon's presence at the altar table serves to symbolise the service to both God and society, in which all are called to participate and the deacon's invitation to the assembly to participate in the sacred mystery reinforces that Christ is indeed present in all the people gathered in his name. However, this theology of the Eucharist can only be appreciated and understood if appropriate formation is provided. Whilst the deacon is cast as an "optional extra" at the Sunday Mass, the fullness of his role in the Eucharist will be devalued. Also, leaving it to local bishops to determine whether or not to have permanent deacons in their dioceses effectively relegates deacons to the margins of sacred ministry.

For personal reflection or for discussion in small groups

1. How would you describe the role of deacon as an "ordinary" minister of Communion?
2. Why do you think it is part of the deacon's role to "co-mingle" the water and the wine at the Offertory?

Endnotes

---

[1] Pope John Paul II 1992. Pastores Dabo Vobis http://www.vatican.va/holy_father/john_paul_ii/apost_exhortations/documents/hf_jp-ii_exh_

25031992_pastores-dabo-vobis_en.html accessed 13/02/2013 – Libreria Editrice Vaticana (© Libreria Editrice Vaticana, 2013).

[2] The site invites "visitors" to go either to the Bishops' Conference site which replicates the sparse materials given in the National Vocations Office site or signposts to the *Deacons Place* web site which is focused on the diaconal community rather than the parishioner.

[3] Catholic Bishops Conference of England and Wales – Liturgy Office 2005. *With Hearts and Minds* – Participants Book London: CTS. p.32

[4] The Roman Missal Jerusalem Bible Version 1973.

12 | Women's Diaconal Ministry

The main focus of the Southwark Province research project was to explore the ecclesial understanding of the role of the permanent diaconate in the contemporary Roman Catholic Church and, in order to do so, it was necessary to situate this restored ministry against the backdrop of its roots in the early Church, trace its development and subsequent suppression and to take note of the Vatican II conciliar debates which informed the decision to restore it. The experience of contemporary deacons in terms of formation and the influence and impact of their ministry upon their family, professional lives and in the parish provided the empirical component of this work. The tensions posed by a threefold ministry of priesthood, two of which require the discipline of celibacy and one which does not, have also been explored.

Consideration was also given to the role of the deacon's spouse, whose approval for her husband's ministry is a necessary pre-requisite for his acceptance for pre-diaconal formation. As the Permanent Diaconate Handbook for the Diocese of Southwark states: "With married deacons, we see an interface and a creative tension between the Sacrament of Marriage and the Sacrament of Orders, both sacraments being enriched and affected by the other".[1] This positive affirmation of the married deacon is juxtaposed with the negativity implicit in the prohibition of marriage for both widowed deacons and those who are single when ordained. The confusion which has arisen from a poorly articulated theology of diaconate is further compounded by equality and gender issues which arise from a ministry which entirely excludes women. This issue cannot simply be ignored. It remains as a large ecclesiological "elephant in the room" which requires at least acknowledgment if not measured debate.[2]

In his apostolic letter *Ordinatio Sacerdotalis* dated May 22 1994, Pope John Paul II reaffirmed the Church's teaching:

> ...in order that all doubt may be removed regarding a matter of great importance, a matter which pertains to the Church's divine constitution itself, in virtue of my ministry of confirming the brethren (cf. Luke 22:32) I declare that the Church has no authority whatsoever to confer priestly ordination on women and that this judgment is to be definitively held by all the Church's faithful (OS4).[3]

For many Catholics and indeed, for those who avow no faith whatever, the exclusion of women from roles of ordained ministry brings the Church into conflict with the aspirations of most modern democracies. Equality before the law now enables women to take their place in professional and commercial life and seeks to protect them against exploitation and oppression. Whilst this is still very much "work in progress", the failure of the Church to acknowledge the need to even debate the issue leaves it open to criticism and derision. It is the intention of this chapter to explore the implications of an exclusively male-gendered permanent diaconate, but this time situate it historically against the experience of women in the early Church, in medieval society and modern times.

In exploring the issue of women's ministry in general and the diaconate in particular, it is helpful to unearth the historical roots of women's ministry in much the same way as the development of the male diaconate was outlined in earlier chapters. This can lead to further reflection on how the call to universal holiness and the ecclesiology of Vatican II can be reconciled with the continued exclusion of women from the Sacrament of Order.

A suitable starting point for exploring this issue is *Priest and Diaconate*, by Archbishop Gerhard Müller, former Bishop of Regensburg who served from 1998-2003 as a member of the International Theological Commission and is now Prefect of the Congregation for the Doctrine of the Faith. His theological credentials identify him as a suitable representative of the

Magisterium for making the case against the ordination of women to the diaconate. Müller's starting point is that:

> Certainly the problem of women in the contemporary Church should not demand the same energy and attention as the question of whether human beings can believe in the existence, presence and incarnation of God in the first place.[4]

Put simply, Müller suggests that the gender and equality "problem" is insignificant when set against the fundamental issue of belief in God and Jesus Christ. The resulting theological conundrum however is that the Church, as a community of believers, attesting to being "Christ in the World" and reading the "signs of the times" dismisses half of the world's population as being ecclesiastical "invalid matter".

In making his argument, Müller cites Pinius's *Acta Sanctorum* written in 1746, in which the latter sets forth Hippolytus's argument from his *Traditio Apostolica 10*, that the bishop in placing his hands on the head of the deaconess is not ordaining her but rather blessing her and argues that "there is not one single pronouncement of the *Magisterium* that would call into question the connection between the sacramental diaconal ministry and baptised males." He asserts that the task of giving an authentic interpretation of the word of God, whether in written form or in the form of Tradition has been entrusted to the living teaching office of the Church alone[5] and that the conferral of Holy Orders on males cannot simply be explained by some "alleged 'unsuitability' that goes with being a woman" but that when God took on human nature, he did so in the masculine mode, although included in this anthropological understanding is the relatedness of male and female.

Müller then argues that by taking on masculinity, "the *Logos* communicates himself with the new people of God in that fundamental personal relationship that has its foundation in masculinity".[6] He then outlines the establishment of the Church, based upon the commissioning of the Twelve, citing Luke 23:34, Acts 1:21, 1 Cor. 15:3-5 and Gal. 1:17. and develops his argument around the institution of the post-apostolic ministries of *episcopoi* and *presbyteroi*. He takes the view that, although there is no doubt about the common vocation of all men and women, apostolic ministry is restricted only to men. He cites 1 Cor. 14:33-37 on the banning of women from speaking in church, although acknowledges that they may hand on the teachings of the faith in the family and in their circle of acquaintances (1 Tim. 3:11, 2 Tim. 1:5 and Tit. 2:4).[7]

Müller argues for the Church's continued observance of a restriction which he registers from the time to Jesus to the present day, calling upon the writings of the early Church fathers – Origen, Irenaeus, Clement of Alexandria, Tertullian and Cyprian, concluding that they all understood the Church to hold a common priesthood of all believers in which all men and women participated, but that the special apostolic ministry of proclaiming the gospel, the administration of sacraments and pastoral ministry, as conferred sacramentally on bishop, presbyter and deacon could only be exercised by men. He recognises that the roles of the widow, the deaconess and those with the charism of prophetic speech existed in the early Church, but these were not ordained ministries. He quotes fourth century Ambrosiaster's explication of 1 Tim. 3:11:

> Because the Apostle addresses women after the deacons, the Cataphrygians[8] seize upon this as an opportunity for heresy and with vain arrogance maintain that the deaconesses too must have been ordained; even though they know that the apostles selected seven men as deacons. Could they not find on that occasion any suitable women since we read that here were holy women with the twelve apostles (Acts 1:14).... Yet the apostle orders women to be silent in the assembly of the faithful.[9]

Moving into the Middle Ages, the *Decretum Gratiani,* in which are assembled those papal writings which became incorporated into the Code of Canon Law, specifically excludes women from either the priesthood or diaconate. The subsequent Codes published in 1917 and 1983 have not revised this position. In summarising the position of the scholastic theologians, and in particular Aquinas, Müller argues that far from being misogynistic, the theologians of this period recognised the equality of women, not least in that both men and women were permitted to baptise *in extremis*. Aquinas acknowledges the charism of prophesy, although this is not regarded as ministry and that women may be superiors in women's religious orders and exercise authority in civic life. He also notes the catechetical role of women in the home but distinguishes this from the teaching authority of the bishops and priests.[10] He declares that even if the external ceremony of ordination is carried out, it would be neither licit nor valid as it would not reflect the will of Christ as manifested in the Church's practice.

Müller concludes by stating that Aquinas does not base his teaching on arguments of suitability but on Scripture, tradition and the Church's doctrine. He marshals an argument based upon the sacramental symbolism of Christ the bridegroom to the Church, his Bride. In order to achieve the symbolic fullness of this dynamic, the priest must be a man. Müller then sweeps up the remaining centuries of the post-Tridentine era up until the mid nineteenth century with the statement:

> ...we find an uncontested unanimity of all the authoritative theologians, an agreement that the teaching about the connection between Holy Orders and the male sex is of divine right and proceeds necessarily from the nature of the Sacrament of Orders as a representation of Christ.[11]

Against the backdrop of this overall position on Holy Orders, Müller then offers his critique on the sacramental diaconate. His starting point is, fittingly, the *diakonia* of Christ and his self-emptying as described in Mark 10:45: "For the Son of Man also came not to be served but to serve and to give his life as a ransom for many".

Like the universal priesthood of all believers, all are called to *diakonia*, but since service is a definitive characteristic of apostolic ministry, diaconal service finds sacramental expression in the diaconate. The ministry of the deacon of the early Church has already been described and Müller's account of this draws upon the same sources i.e. Ignatius, Clement, and Hippolytus. However, he also refers to the role of the *diakonissa/ministra* which he identifies as a non-sacramental office and emphasises that "there is no such thing as an ecclesial office of human origin that participates in some non-sacramental way in the sacramental hierarchy, which consists exclusively of the degrees of bishop, presbyters and deacon". However he concedes that the offices of subdeacon, deaconess and lector have sometimes been defined as clergy and sometimes not.[12]

Müller settles the question by declaring that the redactor of the *Apostolic Constitutions* rejected any possible blending of the ministries of different degrees and that if God had an undifferentiated ministry, it could have been communicated in a single consecration and that not only is ordained ministry in general but its subdivisions of bishop, presbyter and deacon are prescribed by God.[13] He cites the *Apostolic Constitutions 8, 28*, "The deaconess does not bless, nor perform anything belonging to the office of presbyters or deacons, but only is to keep the doors, and to minister to the presbyters in the baptizing of women, on account of decency." In marshalling his final argument, Müller concludes that the diaconal ministry is part of Holy Orders which originates in the salvific mission of Christ and that where diaconal ministries are carried out by laymen, ordination is advisable.

It is difficult for a researcher who is lay person and a woman to read Müller's critique and feel affirmed by it. It is uncompromising and allows for no nuance in interpretation. By his assessment, women can never be considered for any ordained ministry, priestly or diaconal and those diaconal functions which are presently performed by laymen should, if possible, be undertaken in Holy Orders. Using his argument, women cannot be ordained to any echelon within Holy Orders because Christ does not call them to this ministry and never did.

Müller's work effectively articulates the position held by the *Magisterium* and whilst this offers little opportunity for dialogue, it is nonetheless valid for the sake of completeness to offer a counter-argument. For this, the works of Susanne Heine and John Wijngaards will be used. Heine is an Austrian Protestant pastor and professor of practical theology and Wijngaards a former Roman

Catholic priest of the Mill Hill Missionaries, who resigned his priestly ministry because of his opposition to the Church's pronouncements on priestly celibacy, the use of artificial means of birth control and the ordination of women.

In her account of the women's equality argument, Heine cautions against a simplistic acceptance of what is generally perceived to be the feminist position i.e. that male dominated clericalism is a facet of oppressive patriarchalism. She notes that Paul in 1 Cor.14:34 provides a ready target for the feminist lobby. Furthermore, any declared dichotomy of the "male theology of the head" set against the emotion of females presupposes that women are incapable of intellectual discourse. Heine, however, wishes to engage in a more rounded argument which explores both the history and the theology of the role of women in the early Church. She finds that it is difficult to gain a truly historical perspective from writings which are intrinsically theological i.e. the gospels and New Testament Letters and poses some simple fundamental questions:

> Were the women followers of Jesus in the comprehensive way that the disciples were or did they provide financial support and a limited degree of *diakonia* for Jesus and his followers? If we assume…that women and men were followers of Jesus to an equal degree, what does that mean for the present position and function of women in Christian churches?[14]

Heine argues that in the canonically valid texts, Jesus and his praxis are the criteria for the praxis of Christians and lists the following characteristics of the disciples: detached from the traditional forms of society, no fixed abode, no possessions, no mention of family life and lack of clarity around sexual asceticism. She suggests that:

> In the absence of historical information, the norm would be provided by a philosophical and anthropological reflection on humanity. Galatians 3:28 would be that kind of norm even if reality does not match the claim.[15]

For many who support the ordination of women, Galatians 3:28 is indeed an attractive starting point.

Heine then explores the portrayal of Eve, and hence all women, as inherently weak, seductive and unreliable.[16] One of the more chilling condemnations of women is provided by Tertullian's instruction *On the Apparel of Women i.1*. Speaking of Eve he says:

> ...the ignominy, I mean of the first sin and the odium attaching to her as the cause of human perdition. In pains and in anxieties you bear children, woman; and towards your husband is your inclination and he lords it over you. Do you not know that you are each an Eve? The sentence of God on this sex of yours lives in this age; the guilt must of necessity live too. You are the devil's gateway; you are the unsealer of that forbidden tree; you are the deserter of the divine law; you are she who persuaded him whom the devil was not valiant enough to attack. You destroyed so easily God's image, man. On account of your guilt...even the Son of God had to die.[17]

Heine balances this condemnation with other writings, including 1 Cor. 15:21-23, in which it is acknowledged that "Death came through one man and in the same way the resurrection from the dead has come through one man. Just as all men die in Adam, so all men will be brought to life in Christ." She cites Augustine's *Enchiridion* and Cyril of Jerusalem's *Baptismal Catechesis* in which the first **couple** are blamed for the Fall, and not simply Eve on her own. She poses an interpretation of Genesis 3 as a narrative that explains existing practice i.e. the threat of serpents, the pain of childbirth, and the dominance of men over women. These are explained in terms of something which is primeval and mythical. The theological subtext of the myth is that "the dominance of men over women is the consequence of a disruption which goes against God's good will for creation".[18] She reads a further causation into the story in so far as the text of Genesis 3 was written during the reign of King Solomon, many of whose foreign wives brought their religious cults of gods and goddesses to the royal court. The judgment on the king's wicked women can be found in the condemnation of the archetypal evil woman of Genesis 3.

When argued on historical grounds, the New Testament accounts include references to deacons like Phoebe and Susanna. As has already been noted, the ministry of female deacons in the anointing of women in baptismal rites was undertaken on grounds of propriety. Other details of female diaconal ministry in the nascent Church are not easily determined. Paul mentions women as his fellow-workers and a quarter of all the active collaborators mentioned in his letters are female. Heine lists Euodia, Julia, Junias, Mary, Nympha, Persis, Phoebe, Prisca, Syntyche, Tryphaena and Tryposa, most of whom are mentioned in Romans 16:1. Phoebe is named as a deacon and Heine notes that the term is applied in the masculine, thereby suggesting that there was no gender distinction between the early deacons. The title "deaconess" dates from the second century.

In terms of Roman and early Christian history, the official approval of Christianity by the Roman Emperor Constantine in 313, resulted in the adoption of many Roman social norms within the Church communities. Wijngaards highlights the efficiency of Roman law in matters of administration and settling disputes, but sees within it a structural prejudice against women. Within the family, the father had complete authority over his wife and children and, outside the home, women held no civil authority nor rights to appear in court, either as witnesses nor as advocates for their own interests. This prevailing culture percolated into theological thinking, as demonstrated by Ambrosiaster in the fourth century:

> ...women must cover their heads because they are not the image of God...How can anyone maintain that woman is the likeness of God when she is demonstrably subject to the dominion of man and has no kind of authority? For she can neither teach nor be a witness in court nor exercise citizenship nor be a judge – then certainly not exercise dominion.[19]

The ordination rites for deacons in the Byzantine Church of the sixth to eighth centuries i.e. before the Eastern Schism, directly challenge any assertion that the early church women deacons were not actually ordained. Wijngaards lays the rubrics and prayers of the ceremonies for male and female deacons side by side and concludes that they were almost identical. The rubric refers to the "woman who is to be ordained", brought before the bishop, who imposes his hands on her forehead and makes the Sign of the Cross on it three times and asks the Lord to "look on this your maidservant and dedicate her to the ministry *(leitourgia)* of your diaconate and pour out into her the rich and abundant giving of your Holy Spirit".[20] After intercessory prayers, both the male and female deacons have a second laying-on of hands. Over the male deacon, the bishop asks that he is filled through the life-giving coming of the Holy Spirit with all faith, charity, power and holiness. The female deacon's prayer is:

> Grant the gift of your Holy Spirit also to this your maidservant who wants to dedicate herself to you and fulfil in her the grace of the ministry of the diaconate as you granted to Phoebe the grace of your diaconate, Phoebe whom you had called to the work of the ministry *(leitourgia)*.

The deacons are then invested with the stole as their official vestment, the male deacon given the thurible with which to incense the gifts for the first time. Both female and male deacons are handed the chalice containing particles of the consecrated bread immersed in the consecrated blood, the male deacons to distribute it in the assembly and the female deacons to bring it to the sick. Wijngaards concludes that the rites were identical under parallel invocations of the Holy Spirit and adds as a wry coda Canon 4 of the Council of Trent:

> If anyone says that through sacred ordination, the Holy Spirit is not given, and that therefore the Bishop says in vain "Receive the Holy Spirit" or that through this ordination the character [of Holy Orders] is not imprinted... Let him be anathema.[21]

In summarising the influence of the Scholastic theologians and canonists, Wijngaards tabulates his findings as follows:

Opinion or view expressed	Medieval theologians who held this view	Medieval theologians who presented this explicitly as an argument against the ordination of women
Women are inferior to men by nature	Gratian, Bandinelli, Sicardus, Huguccio, Teutonicau	Aquinas, Bonaventure, Middleton, Scotus, Durandus
Women are not created in the image of God as men are	Gratian, Aquinas, de Sergusio	Huguccio, Bonaventure, de Baysio, de Butrio
Women still carry the burden of Eve's sin	Gratian, Sicardus, Teutonicus	Huguccio, de Baysio
Women are not perfect human beings and thus cannot represent Christ		Aquinas, Bonaventure, Andrae
Paul forbids women to teach in church or to have authority over men	Gratian, de Sergusio	Aquinas, Bonaventure, Middleton, Scotus, Durandus, Andrae
Christ did not include a woman among the apostolic twelve. There were only men at the Last Supper		de Sergusio, Middleton, Scotus, Durandus
Women cannot be ordained because it is forbidden by the Church		Bonaventure, Rufinus, Huguccio, Teutonicus

Wijngaards tests these arguments against current Church documents and concludes that the assertions that women are not created in the image of God, as men are, and that they are subservient to men are no longer valid. Similarly, the argument that they still carry the burden of Eve's sin is no longer supported. The injunction that they may not teach in church is still, however, regarded as valid, as is the main argument against ordination of women that Jesus did not include a woman among the apostolic twelve. The assertion that women cannot represent Christ is therefore still valid.

Wijngaards explains that the *Magisterium* asserts that because Christ was a man, only a man can represent him properly[22] and he speculates that it might be argued that only those who resemble first century Jewish men could rightfully take their place at the altar. If, however the priest is a symbolic representation of Christ, then all who have been "baptised into Christ"(Gal.3:26) carry his image, as they are indeed a new creation (2 Cor. 5:17).

Pope Paul VI's encyclical *Inter Insigniores* explains that because of the relationship of Christ the bridegroom with the Church as his Bride, the priest who is *in persona Christi* must be male –

> … therefore, unless one is to disregard the importance of this symbolism for the economy of Revelation, it must be admitted that, in actions which demand the character of ordination and in which Christ himself, the author of the Covenant, the Bridegroom, the Head of the Church, is represented, exercising his ministry of salvation- which is in the highest degree the case of the Eucharist- his role (this is the original sense of the word 'persona') must be taken by a man (*Inter Insigniores* 5).[23]

This is further developed in Pope John Paul II's encyclical *Mulieris Dignitatem*, given in 1988, in which is stated:

> It is the Eucharist above all that expresses the redemptive act of Christ the Bridegroom towards the Church the Bride. This is clear and unambiguous when the sacramental ministry of the Eucharist, in which the priest acts "in persona Christi", is performed by a man (*Mulieris Dignitatem* 26).[24]

Couched in these terms, Eucharist takes on the overtones of coitus rather than sacrificial outpouring. Hans Urs Von Balthasar explains the Eucharistic mystery in terms which are overtly sexual:

> The priestly ministry and the sacrament are means of passing on seed. They are a male preserve. They aim at inducing in the Bride her function as a woman.[25]

and in *Elucidations,* published in 1975, he speaks of:

> What else is his Eucharist but, at a higher level, an endless act of fruitful outpouring of his whole flesh, such as a man can only achieve for a moment with a limited organ of his body?

Beattie finds this explication of Eucharist to be based upon the uniquely male experience of penile ejaculation rather than an identification with Christ's death. Within this understanding, she sees women as bystanders in the:

> ...metaphysical consummation of homosexual love, a marriage between men and God in which the male body is both the masculine bridegroom and the feminine bride, the masculine God and the feminine creature, the masculine Christ and the feminine Church.[26]

Sullivan's *Afterword*

In terms of the way forward, the case for the institution of a female diaconate is difficult to sustain against the burden of history and theological and canonical intractability. In bringing this Women's Chapter to a close, it is perhaps fruitful to bring the insights of Francis Sullivan to bear on the document with which the chapter began, the apostolic letter of Pope John Paul II, *Ordinatio Sacerdotalis* dated May 22 1994. In an Afterword to his 1995 work *Creative Fidelity*, Sullivan explains that he initially regarded the teaching of the apostolic letter to be in the category of ordinary papal teaching i.e. not infallibly defined. However on November 1995, the Congregation of the Doctrine of the Faith (CDF) issued a declaration to the effect that the doctrine excluding women from ordination to the priesthood pertains to the deposit of faith and that it has been infallibly taught by the ordinary and universal *magisterium*. Sullivan explains that to be part of the "deposit of faith" means that it has been revealed by God, but Sullivan passes the task of explaining the grounds for such a statement to the scripture scholars. Instead he explores what it means to have the document carry the weight of the "ordinary and universal *magisterium*". He explains that Catholic theologians have commonly taught that there are some articles of faith which have never been solemnly defined but which nonetheless have been infallibly taught by the ordinary and universal *magisterium*. However this document from the Holy See is the first one to have been infallibly taught in this way. For Sullivan, this implies that it is a clearly established fact that the world-wide episcopate is in agreement with the pope that the exclusion of women from ordination to the priesthood is a divinely revealed doctrine and one which must be held definitively by all the faithful.[27] Sullivan questions how the CDF know that this **is** an established fact and adds that the CDF's statement is not infallible because, even if published with papal approval, it remains a statement of the Congregation to which the pope cannot give his prerogative of infallibility. Sullivan elucidates that, when a doctrine is infallibly taught, it is irreversible. Its meaning can be clarified in further developments but it cannot be reversed. Sullivan then gives a few examples where the "further developments" resulted in the doctrine no longer being held as the teaching of the Church – the Council of Florence's declaration in 1442 that all pagans and Jews would be condemned to hell if they did not become Catholics before they died, and the doctrine which held that it was morally permissible to own slaves.

In seeking to establish the views of the ordinary and universal *magisterium*, the pope may call upon the college of bishops worldwide or seek the consensus of Catholic theologians or be aware of the *sensus fidelium* in the matter i.e. the common adherence of the faithful to an article of faith. Sullivan notes that the CDF did not invoke any of these criteria in the matter of the ordination of women priests and he concludes:

> The question that remains in my mind is whether it is a clearly established fact that the bishops of the Catholic Church are as convinced by those reasons as Pope John Paul II evidently is and that, in exercising their proper role as judges and teachers of the faith, they have been unanimous in teaching that the exclusion of women from ordination to the priesthood is a divinely revealed truth to which all Catholics are obliged to give a definitive assent of faith. Unless this is manifestly the case, I do not see how it can be certain that this doctrine

has been taught infallibly by the ordinary and universal *magisterium*.[28]

Prospective female deacons

The reflections of prospective female deacons and others with an interest in this ministry have been captured in Ratigan and Swidler's A *New Phoebe – Perspectives on Roman Catholic Women and the Permanent Diaconate*.[29] The contributors to the publication include wives of deacons, two bishops and prospective female deacons who undertook the full diaconal programme but were disbarred from ordination with their male peers. The accounts are as hopeful as they are sad, with many of the contributors deeply involved in diaconal service, but without the official affirmation of Holy Orders. Ratigan and Swidler explain that, even as an exclusively male-gendered ministry, the diaconate is still regarded by some as an expedient to address shortages of priests and therefore diverts from the real issue – mandatory celibacy. One of the priest contributors to their findings criticises deacons "who have become more clericalised than the very priests with whom they serve…and seem more comfortable dressed in albs than in leadership roles in the community".[30] One of the contributors who felt called to ordained diaconal ministry admitted feeling anger about her exclusion on grounds of gender. She explained:

> I believe that women bring another dimension to ministry and another outlook to preaching. We image our God in other ways that can be helpful to people. Sometimes I feel that I don't want to buy into the system which I feel is seriously flawed, but another part of me says that the reformers need to get as many noses in the tent as possible to effect change.[31]

In summary therefore, so long as the permanent diaconate is regarded as part of the threefold ministry of ordained priesthood, it is difficult to envisage a time when women may be admitted to Holy Orders in the Catholic Church. If, on the other hand, diaconate is redefined as a separate ministry which does not carry the problematic "ordination" word, and which stands outside the threefold priestly ministry, there may yet be hope for women to have a conferral of sacramental grace upon their service.

The experience of many women in the contemporary Church is that they are, indeed, living diaconal lives in their modes of service and their mode of prayer. In service to the word, they are involved in catechesis, sacramental preparation and children's liturgy of the word. Regarding the latter, although the proclamation of the Gospel within Mass is reserved to the priest celebrant or the deacon, its proclamation to the children in children's liturgy of the word is undertaken by lay people, both male and female. Common practice shows that the majority of parish catechists are women. Their contribution in works of charity to the sick, housebound and bereaved is readily evidenced in parish care groups. Extraordinary Ministers of Holy Communion provide sacramental ministry as bearers of Holy Communion from the Sunday Eucharist and include proclamation of the word as part of their visitation. In terms of function therefore, it is difficult to sustain an argument which excludes women from an echelon of Holy Orders whilst the functions carried out in the name of the Church are almost identical to those of their ordained male counterparts.

Conscious of the celebrations for the Year of Faith, one can perhaps imagine the conversation which might occur between a parent and a teenage son who declares that he feels called to priesthood. The prayers and encouragement offered to support him might well be matched only by the parents' pride and joy at his ordination. A parallel conversation with a daughter would, by the *Magisterium's* argument, draw a response that she could not possibly be called by Jesus to serve him in Holy Orders and if she wishes to remain a Roman Catholic, she should consider the matter closed. In the light of magisterial intractability, an alternative replay of the scenario for the young man's vocational conversation might now include an observation that since the Church has offered poor validation for its stance on sacred ministry, he might do well to seriously reconsider the life to which he presently feels called.

Recent developments

On 26 October 2009, Pope Benedict XVI issued *Omnium in Mentem*, a brief *motu proprio*[32] document clarifying canon law in respect of the diaconate and priesthood. The amended Canon 1008 would affirm that "those who receive the sacrament of orders are destined to serve the People of God with a new and specific title" rather than "fulfilling in the person of Christ the Head, the functions of teaching, sanctifying, and governing" (Can. 1008). Canon 1009 which simply lists the three orders as episcopate, priesthood and diaconate, would be further amplified by an additional paragraph drawing a distinction between the priestly orders (episcopate and priesthood), wherein are received the mission and power to act in the person of Christ and the diaconal order which receives the faculty to serve the people of God in the diaconates of the liturgy, of the word and of charity. This canonical development may signal a willingness to consider the possibility of admitting women to the ordained ministry of permanent deacon. Zagano[33] takes the view that this new distinction made between priesthood and diaconate helps to address the misunderstanding that the diaconate was a transitional vocation on the way to priesthood. She also recalls that Pope Paul VI had requested a clarification of the theological issues around a female diaconate but that the International Theological Commission took thirty years to produce its report. Zagano suggests that since Pope Benedict XVI was a member of the commission, "he cannot forget Paul's question". In summary, by making a clear canonical distinction between the sacred orders, the *motu proprio* could signal the restoration of women to the ancient order of deacon.

For personal reflection or for discussion in small groups

1. How might women be affirmed in their Church ministry without seeking the conferral of the sacramental grace of Holy Orders?
2. How would you explain to a non-Catholic the Church's position on the exclusion of women from sacred orders?

Endnotes

---

¹ Diocese of Southwark 1994. *The Permanent Diaconate in the Diocese of Southwark.*

² The decision of the Lambeth Conference in 1968 to admit Anglican women to the diaconate, the gradual acceptance of the ordination of women to the priesthood within the Anglican communion and the admittance of women to priestly orders in other Christian denominations remain in sharp relief to the position maintained by the Roman Catholic Church that the exclusion of women from Holy Orders was directed by Jesus himself.

³ Pope John Paul II 1994. *Ordinatio Sacerdotalis* http://www.vatican.va/holy_father/john_paul_ii/apost_letters/documents/hf_jp-ii_apl_22051994_ordinatio-sacerdotalis_en.html accessed 12/02/2013 – Libreria Editrice Vaticana (© Libreria Editrice Vaticana, 2013).

⁴ Muller, G. 2002. *Priesthood and Diaconate.* San Francisco: Ignatius Press.p.23.

⁵ Ibid p.64.

⁶ Ibid p.108-9.

⁷ Ibid.p.146.

⁸ The Cataphrygians were an off-shoot of the heretical Montanists who lived in the territory of Phrygia from which their name is derived.

⁹ Muller, G. 2002. *Priesthood and Diaconate.* San Francisco: Ignatius Press p.155.

¹⁰ *Summa Theologiae* 2-2, 177, 2 Objection 2. Further, the grace of prophesy is greater than the grace of the word, even as the contemplation of truth is greater than its utterance. But prophecy is granted to women, as we read of Deborah (Judges 4:4), and of Holda the prophetess, the wife of Sellum (2 Kings 22:14), and of the four daughters of Philip (Acts 21:9). Moreover the Apostle says (1Corinthians 11:5): "Every woman praying or prophesying," etc. Much more therefore would it seem that the grace of the word is becoming to a woman. http://www.newadvent.org/summa/3177.htm accessed 19/11/ 2009

¹¹ Muller, G. 2002. *Priesthood and Diaconate.* San Francisco: Ignatius Press d.p.175.

¹² Canon 19 of the Council of Nicea, in dealing with the re-baptism of the Paulianists who have been received into the Church "Likewise in the case of their deaconesses, and generally in the case of those who have been enrolled among their clergy, let the same form be observed. And we mean

by deaconesses such as have assumed the habit, but who, since they have no imposition of hands, are to be numbered only among the laity. http://www.newadvent.org/ fathers/3801.htm accessed 20/11/2009
However, in Book III of the *Apostolic Constitutions* Section 2 is entitled "On Deacons and Deaconesses, the Rest of the Clergy" and states "Ordain also a deaconess who is faithful and holy, for the ministrations towards women. For sometimes he cannot send a deacon, who is a man, to the women, on account of unbelievers. You shall therefore send a woman, a deaconess, on account of the imaginations of the bad. For we stand in need of a woman, a deaconess, for many necessities; and first in the baptism of women, the deacon shall anoint only their forehead with the holy oil, and after him the deaconess shall anoint them: for there is no necessity that the women should be seen by the men.." http://www.newadvent.org/cathen/15687b.htm accessed 20/11/2009

[13] Muller, G. 2002. *Priesthood and Diaconate*. San Francisco: Ignatius Press. p.207.

[14] Heine, S. 1987. *Women and Early Christianity*. English translation by J Bowden. London: SCM. p.7.

[15] Ibid. p.9.

[16] During instruction, a woman should be quiet and respectful. I am not giving permission for a woman to teach or to tell a man what to do. A woman ought not to speak, because Adam was formed first and Eve afterwards, and it was not Adam who was led astray but the woman who was led astray and fell into sin, Nevertheless, she will be saved by childbearing, provided she lives a modest life and is constant in faith and love and holiness" 1 Tim. 2:11-15

[17] Heine, S. 1987. Women and Early Christianity. English translation by J Bowden. London: SCM. p.16.

[18] Ibid. p.21.

[19] Ambrosiaster on 1.Cor 14, 34 in Wijngaards, J. 2001. *The Ordination of Women in the Catholic Church – Unmasking a Cuckoo's Egg Tradition*. London: Darton Longman and Todd. p.53

[20] Extract from Wijngaards, J. 2001. *The Ordination of Women in the Catholic Church – Unmasking a Cuckoo's Egg Tradition*. London: Darton Longman and Todd. See also http://www.womendeacons.org/discussion/deac_ord.shtml accessed 13/02/2013

[21] Council of Trent Canon 4. http://history.hanover.edu/texts/trent/ct23.html accessed 13/02/13

²² Pope Paul VI. 1976. *Declaration On The Question Of Admission Of Women To The Ministerial Priesthood Inter Insigniores* October 15, 1976 http://www.papalencyclicals.net/Paul06/p6interi.htm "The Christian priesthood is therefore of a sacramental nature: the priest is a sign, the supernatural effectiveness of which comes from the ordination received, but a sign that must be perceptible and which the faithful must be able to recognise with ease. The whole sacramental economy is in fact based upon natural signs, on symbols imprinted on the human psychology: 'Sacramental signs,' says St.Thomas,' represent what they signify by natural resemblance.' The same natural resemblance is required for persons as for things: when Christ's role in the Eucharist is to be expressed sacramentally, there would not be this 'natural resemblance' which must exist between Christ and his minister if the role of Christ were not taken by a man: in such a case it would be difficult to see in the minister the image of Christ. For Christ himself was and remains a man." accessed 23/11/2009

²³ Pope Paul VI 1976. *Inter Insigniores* http://www.vatican.va/roman_curia/congregations/cfaith/documents/rc_con_cfaith_doc_19761015_inter-insigniores _en.html accessed 13/02/2013 – Libreria Editrice Vaticana (© Libreria Editrice Vaticana, 2013).

²⁴ Pope John Paul II 1988. *Mulieris Dignitatem.* http://www.vatican.va/holy_father/john_paul_ii/apost_letters/documents/hf_jp-ii_apl_15081988_mulieris-dignitatem_en.html accessed 13/02/2013 - Libreria Editrice Vaticana (© Libreria Editrice Vaticana, 2013).

²⁵ This quotation is ascribed to Von Balthasar's 1965 publication *Wer ist Kirche?* Vier Skizzen, Freiburg p 24.

²⁶ Beattie, T. in Wijngaards, J. 2001. *The Ordination of Women in the Catholic Church – Unmasking a Cuckoo's Egg Tradition.* London:Darton Longman and Todd. p.120.

²⁷ Pottmeyer, H. 1998. *Towards a Papacy in Communion.* English translation by M.J. O'Connell. New York: Crossroad Publishing Company. p.117-128.

²⁸ Sullivan, F.A. 1996. *Creative Fidelity.* Dublin: Gill and Macmillan. p. 184.

²⁹ Ratigan, V.K., A.A. Swidler (eds) 1990. *A New Phoebe – Perspectives on Roman Catholic Wonmen and the Permanent Diaconate.* Kansas City: Sheed and Ward.

³⁰ Ibid. p.5.

³¹ Ibid. p.30.

[32] A *motu proprio* document is one which is issued by the pope on his own authority and not at the request of others.
[33] Zagano, P. 2010. "Inching towards a 'Yes'". *The Tablet.* 9 January 2010.

13 | SUMMARY AND THE WAY AHEAD

In this closing chapter, I will provide some headlines for the issues which have been discussed in the earlier chapters. I will also plot a trajectory for the future of the permanent diaconate and some possible areas for further research.

It is clear that the Second Vatican Council which restored the permanent diaconate provided a profoundly different ecclesiological context in which the permanent deacons would serve – namely in a community of believers now called the "People of God" or a "Pilgrim People" mandated by Baptism to participate fully in the work of the Kingdom of God. It is, therefore, not helpful to regard the contemporary permanent diaconate as merely a restored ancient ministry, but one which is located within, and responsive to, a contemporary Church context.

I have chosen three main headings for presenting the research findings: Scripture, Ecclesiology (the branch of theology which explores Church structure and self-understanding) and Pastoral Practice.

Scripture

Although Acts 6 has generally been regarded as the foundational biblical text for diaconal ministry, both ancient and modern, fresh insights supplied by contemporary theologians like John Collins, invite a more comprehensive consideration of *diakonia*, one which acknowledges the covenantal underpinning of Deuteronomy and Exodus, as noted in the works of Johnson and Witherington in Chapter 1. As a Christian value, *diakonia* permeates all aspects of the lives of believers and cannot be exclusively assigned to those in Holy Orders. Instead, the deacon symbolises service to word, sacrament and works of charity to which all the faithful are called and he represents this value within the Sacrament of Order. Within this interpretation, there is no false dichotomy between the sacred and the secular since the lay faithful are themselves called to be "religious in the world".[1] Collins urges deacons to revisit, not only Acts 6 but also Acts 1:8 in which Peter invites the followers to find a replacement for Judas' *diakonia*, and also the accounts in Mark 10, Matthew 25 and Luke's use of table fellowship as the symbol of the presence of God. Seen in this light, the ministry of the deacon becomes more than social service offered in the name of the Church, but a symbolic representation of the *diakonia* of Christ to which all are called. Cast in this role, the deacon is less likely to be perceived as a limited functionary, permitted to undertake relatively minor liturgical roles ostensibly to shore up a presbyterate, which, in terms of numbers, appears to be in decline.[2]

In applying the research question directly to the scriptural interpretation of *diakonia*, the empirical evidence from Southwark Province points to a developing appreciation among lay faithful of the deacon's ministry, based mainly on his pastoral practice, rather than insights derived from recent scripture studies. The feedback from the deacons on their own comprehension of their ministry evidences an appreciation of a complex multi-layered ministry which is far from the "table-waiting" social service which a simplistic reading of Acts 6 may suggest. The challenge for the leader within the ecclesial community is to ensure that the fullest and richest interpretation of the deacon's ministry is recognised, so that he is an empowering animator of faith and a catalyst for service within the community.

Ecclesiology

Having widened the scope of the scriptural interpretation of the deacon's role, it can now be more appropriately evaluated within the Second Vatican Council's motif of the People of God and in relation to the episcopate as the "fullness of order".

The People of God ecclesiology of Vatican II has produced a rich harvest of lay ecclesial ministry and offers the modern Church an inclusive and diverse self-image, one in which all believers are empowered to a full participation in the work of the Kingdom. This

| Summary and the Way Ahead

has implications for both the permanent diaconate and the presbyterate in terms of local leadership and empowerment. It is of course acknowledged that, in institutional terms, participation varies in kind and degree, depending upon the vocation to which each individual is called.[3]

The deacon's participation in the threefold ministry of priesthood

Fifty years after the restoration of the diaconate as a permanent ministry within the threefold order of priesthood, there is still lack of clarity about what the deacon is called to be or to do. The sacramental relationship between the deacon and the bishop is not made explicit in roles which link the diaconate to the episcopate and the relationship between the diaconate and the presbyterate can be similarly problematic. As a result, the deacon may be regarded as a second-rate priest in sacramental provision. Some respondents to the research questionnaire identified their role as one of "filling in gaps" when the priest was overstretched or being a first responder or safety net supporting frail presbyters. Whilst these roles contribute to the overall wellbeing of the faith community, they can "prevent the diaconate from developing its own unique identity and purpose as a legitimate and beneficial order among the people of God."[4]

Foundational to the identity of the permanent deacon is the ontological change brought about through ordination. As an ordained minister, the deacon is a member of a clerical group which is sacramentally "marked" by the conferral of Holy Orders. Whether he exercises his ministry or not, he is sacramentally configured to Christ in a way which lay people are not.[5] It is, therefore, inappropriate to regard the deacon as a layman with an additional mandate for ministry or as "semi-lay" because he is a family man or has a secular profession. In this regard, ordained ministry is not graduated. Bishops are not more ordained than presbyters, who, in turn, are not more ordained than deacons. The evidence from Southwark Province indicates that this understanding of their ontologically changed state is fundamental to the deacons' self-understanding and gives their entire lives a ministerial dimension. Simply put, a deacon is a deacon whether he is at the altar, the office or mowing his lawn. One respondent expressed it as follows, "I feel I am most a deacon when I am not being a deacon."

The distinction between lay and clerical may indeed cause discomfiture in lay people, particularly those who undertake duties which the deacon performs e.g. catechesis or chaplaincy. Given the plethora of lay ecclesial ministry in the contemporary church and the equal rights lobby for women, it could be argued that diaconate as a "mandated" ministry rather than an ordained ministry would release the giftedness of more lay people than the permanent diaconate can achieve. The perceived "superiority" of ordination may therefore serve to dampen the response of lay faithful to pastoral shortages.

As the lay faithful become more theologically literate, it could also be argued that, in terms of resource costs, investment in lay formation would yield a higher "pastoral return" than permanent diaconate formation. These arguments, however, are difficult to sustain when faced with the reality of the selfless dedication of the deacon and his family. Without the sacramental grace and (possibly) the status of Holy Orders, lay faithful may well struggle to justify such radical self-giving to their families, their work colleagues and even themselves.

The challenge of the *Cursus Honorum*

The ordination of "transitional" deacons one year before their ordination to the priesthood helps to reinforce the *Cursus Honorum* in a way which may devalue the ministry of the permanent deacon. For the aspirant priest, the diaconate is a stage of development through which he is graduates en route to the priesthood, rather like a form of ecclesiastical adolescence. The permanent deacon who remains at the "lower level of the hierarchy" can therefore be perceived as a poor compromise for the priest. At its simplest, two members of Holy Orders with divergent ministries bear the same name, one for a limited period and one permanently. The permanent deacon may hold public office but the "transitional" deacon may not. The minimum age requirement for the transitional deacon is twenty-four years old[6] whilst for the permanent deacon it is thirty-five years. Arguably, the "transitional" deacon is ordained to a ministry to which he does not feel called[7] and the integrity of the role of the permanent deacon may be compromised as a result. The "fullness of order" resides in the episcopate, with the presbyterate and diaconate representing the two "arms" of the bishop's ministry to his people. Seen in this light, the transitional diaconate may now be seen to lack credibility and integrity. It is outside the scope of this book to explore the theological significance of the diaconate as a "transitional" clerical state, but it is nonetheless appropriate to highlight the need for clarification. Just as the minor orders[8] and the sub-diaconate, were suppressed after Vatican II, it may now be appropriate to explore how the transitional diaconate contributes fruitfully to the integrated whole of sacred order.

Role of social intermediary

Whilst the collegial aspects of episcopacy have been well articulated in the Vatican II documents, a definitive explication of what the "fullness of order" actually means remains elusive. It has been noted that, for some priests this continues to raise fundamental questions about their participation in a priestly ministry which is, by implication, incomplete. The evidence from Southwark Province indicates that the deacons, although clearly recognising that they are configured sacramentally to the bishop, are unclear how this relationship is made manifest in their diaconal ministry. A minority of respondents have indicated an explicit relationship with the bishop in his role of governance through duties which directly relate to diocesan office but the majority expressed the relationship in non-specific terms like: "They (priests and bishop) are my mentors" or saw themselves as "a bridge between the people and the priest and bishop – if they need a bridge." Some however were not entirely sure how their ministry related to the episcopacy – "I do not have much to do with the bishop" or "I am not sure how it (diaconal ministry) complements the ministry of the bishop." The research evidence suggests that more explicit links with the ministry of the bishop would help consolidate the deacon's role as a full and separate order and one which identifies his sacramental mandate as one from the episcopate, rather than the presbyterate.

In the feedback from the deacons of Southwark Province, there is ample evidence to indicate that they already perform roles of social mediation in their work with the marginalized i.e. refugees, asylum seekers and the vulnerable within the local community. Many cited membership of church-based charities, others represented the Catholic community in *Churches Together* and similar fora, whilst some held positions on civic bodies advocating for the common good. There was, however, no evidence that the wealth of information gleaned from this type of outreach was systematically relayed to bishops in order to inform diocesan pastoral priorities, nor was the relationship defined in theological terms.[9] An area for possible future development arising from the present research is the exploration of suitable mechanisms for permanent deacons to contribute to social and pastoral profiling of their communities so that this intelligence can be directly applied to the allocation of resources to unmet needs. There is, of course, no suggestion that presbyters should be excluded from this exercise, but it is recognised that the deacon, with his direct episcopal mandate for works of charity is perhaps better placed to articulate the community's needs in this regard. By virtue of his ability to hold public office, he also well placed to carry out the bishop's mandate in civic settings which are inaccessible to the presbyter.

Pastoral practice

With regard to ministry of the word, and specifically catechesis and sacramental preparation, the deacons of Southwark Province are mostly engaged in ministry to adults. Some respondents have identified this as a feature of their mature age and their reduced level of interaction with the young. Anecdotal evidence confirms that, indeed, many parish catechists engaged in sacramental programmes designed for young children, particularly First Holy Communion programmes, are female. As shown in Chapter 7, the deacons are heavily engaged in baptismal and marriage preparation programmes and RCIA (Rite for the Christian Initiation of Adults). In respect of their liturgical duties, 73.6% of respondents are involved in proclaiming the gospel and preaching, 32% preside at funerals and 35.8% officiate at marriages. These findings indicate that the deacons have found a stable "niche" for their ministry within their communities.

Deacons and sacramental anointing

It was found that chaplaincy roles also feature prominently in the deacons' repertoire of duties, with hospitals as the predominant setting for this ministry. However, this privileged opportunity to provide pastoral ministry to those who are sick is frustrated by the limitations placed upon the deacon chaplain in respect of the Sacrament of the Sick and the Sacrament of Reconciliation.[10] This deficit is one example of what Osborne refers to as "glaring pastoral need" which is not being addressed[11] and highlights the 1994 request made to the National Conference of Catholic Bishops (NCCB) by the US National Association of Diaconate Directors to petition Rome for permission to allow deacons to become extraordinary ministers of anointing. No action was taken in this regard.

It is outside the scope of this research to examine the canonical and theological implications of permitting the deacon to administer the Sacrament of Reconciliation, the Sacrament of the Sick or a form of sacramental healing. It is however appropriate to highlight the need to explore this matter further. Osborne himself takes the view that the theology of the sacraments was a theological interpretation of the practice of the time and, in the case of the sacrament of anointing of the sick, this became associated exclusively with the forgiveness of sin and the imminence of death only from the twelfth century onwards. He sees no good reason why the theology of sacraments should be confined within the strictures of past practice[12] and strongly advocates that the deacons should at least be considered as "extraordinary" ministers of the Sacrament of the Sick in the manner recommended in Cyprian's Epistle 12.1, alluded to in Chapter 2.

Diaconal marriage

Whilst the empirical data indicates that the deacon's marriage and family life contribute to the richness of his ministry, there is little evidence that this contribution is fully acknowledged or honoured in a meaningful way within the infrastructures of the dioceses. There is no formal affirmation of the spouse's role, apart from the need to have her initial approval at the propaedeutic[13] stage of her husband's formation. Although the concept of "diaconal couple" remains elusive in the UK diaconate, it is becoming more prominent in the USA[14] with resources available for parishes to explore how the deacon's wife may feel called to participate in her husband's ministry. Chapter 8 pointed to Rahner's affirmation of marriage as objectively representing the love of God in Christ for his Church and Kasper's explication of marriage and family life as "the Church in miniature" was also referred to in this section. Cumming's critique of "diaconal marriage" included the sacramental parallels of the ordination and marriage ceremonies. He concluded, however, that the discomfiture which may be felt about married deacons and the role of their spouses arises from a reluctance to acknowledge that "human sexuality is of God and is not without the presence of God"[15] and that this should be the starting point for a fuller understanding of diaconal marriage.

Using Latcovich's model of diaconal role-making and role-taking (Chapters 9 and 10), it was also found that the imposition of the discipline of celibacy on widowed deacons served to reinforce the traditional image of the clergyman as a celibate priest-like figure and that this perhaps posed a challenge to the full acceptance of the deacon's spouse as a partner in his ministry, characterising her merely as an unwelcome appendage to his clerical calling. Whilst it is acknowledged that the prohibition of remarriage for widower deacons honours ancient church tradition (1 Timothy 3:12, Titus 1:6),[16] it could be argued that other stipulations which were applied in the early Church would not be countenanced today e.g. the ordering of slaves to be obedient to their masters (Titus 2:9).

From the testimonies of the married deacons, it is clear that the reservations expressed by parishioners in the 1970s, with regard to married men vested and within the sanctuary, no longer prevail. Also, with the recent introduction of married Roman Catholic priests, the stock knowledge of the Roman Catholic cleric is being further modified and developed. This may serve to broaden the scope for joint ministry for deacons and their wives. The Director of Diaconal Formation for Southwark Province has confirmed that the current diaconate formation programme includes input for deacons' wives and encourages them, if they are able (including those who are not Catholics), to come to formation days. In order to take this aspect of joint diaconal ministry forward, formators of deacons would need to address issues of confidentiality in pastoral ministry and also be sensitive to any discomfiture which might be felt by some presbyters at the prospect of including the deacon's spouse in a more prominent role in the parish.

Framing a Eucharistic context for the diaconate

It has been noted, in both the empirical findings and in the theological reflection, that there is a need for high quality catechesis, religious education and formation in order to frame a Eucharistic context for the diaconate. This is particularly pressing at a time when the restoration of the Extraordinary Rite may send ambiguous signals about the role of the permanent deacon in the liturgical life of the Church. It is recommended, therefore, that future episcopal teaching documents on the Eucharist include a comprehensive account of the theology of the diaconate, as symbolised in the deacon's ministry to the assembly at the Eucharistic celebration. If the deacon's ministry is truly foundational to the identity of the church community, both practically and symbolically, the deacon's presence at the altar for the community's main Eucharistic celebration (Sunday Mass) is essential. If his contribution to the life of the parish is normative, then he can no more be absent from the Eucharistic table than the priest who presides or the congregation. The randomness of his current ministry serves merely to underscore his role as an "optional extra", rather than an essential liturgical embodiment of Christ the Servant.

In terms of the deacon's other liturgical duties, it is recommended that future catechetical materials elaborate the deacon's role, particularly in sacramental preparation for Baptism, Matrimony and the liturgical celebrations at which the deacon may preside i.e. funerals, Benediction and Liturgy of the Hours. Similarly, the deacon's role in works of charity, calls for elucidation, since many of his works in this regard are not undertaken within his parish community. It is essential that formation, religious education and catechesis ensure that the people of God are developed to understand the dynamic role of the deacon, and that he symbolises in the sacrament of order what all are called to be – icons of Christ the Servant. In this regard, he is an animator of the faithful's response to pastoral need and a herald for social justice.

Women's ministry

As a coda to the project, the research also highlighted a parallel strand of discourse with regard to a diaconate ministry for women. Many diaconal duties in catechesis and pastoral care are currently undertaken by women, who are, of course, ineligible for ordination as deacons and yet may seek the sacramental affirmation that comes from Holy Orders. The literature search for the project included an exploration of the role of the deaconess in the early Church. The argument that they were not really "ordained", but merely commissioned, does little to address what some women feel is a systemic misogyny within the Church which should find no place in the third millennium. Although the issue of women's ministry was not the primary purpose of this research, it was impossible to ignore a subject which impacts, not only on deacons' wives, but on laywomen generally. In terms of gender equality, it is an area of dissonance between the church's *Magisterium* and prevailing culture, particularly as it is a topic which still may not be discussed within the Church. However, in the light of canonical clarification[17] on the distinction between the deacon and the priest i.e. the deacon as a minister of service and the priest "*in persona Christi*", there may yet be opportunities for women to be granted the diaconal stole. However, to some, this will still represent a poor concession in the cause of full equality.

Models of leadership

It was noted from the research data that, since there are few opportunities for joint formation and training of priests and deacons, the potential for developing models of collaborative leadership are severely curtailed. Such models would ensure that the gifts of the deacon fully complement those of the presbyter, and that both ministers can then confidently call forth the giftedness of the lay faithful. Such a dynamic inter-relationship would alleviate the anxiety of some lay ministers that their roles are being supplanted by the deacon, or the anxiety of the presbyter that the deacon has been placed there by the bishop "to spy on him". It would also ensure that the "omnivorous priesthood" does not mutate and become an omnivorous diaconate which dominates all local structures and pastoral initiatives. Wilson expresses the need for such formation in *Clericalism, the Death of Priesthood*, when he says:

> 'Leadership' is not a term coming from the big, bad, secular, nasty world of *business*. It is a human issue. It is a necessary component of any human enterprise and, if it is not attended to, the energies of many good people will be wasted and the message of the kingdom distorted.[18]

Wilson suggests a model of leadership which commits "to stay at the table with the community, confronting the reality whatever that reality is." He takes the view that leadership is about "wholes" not "parts" and that pastoral leaders must bring the energies of the community together rather than letting them fragment and dissipate. He also urges leaders to have the security to trust their delegated officers since they cannot do everything. Citing Edwin Friedman's description of the good leader as a "non-anxious presence", Wilson suggests that:

> ...a good leader emanates confidence that the people have the capacity to confront even the most complex realities constructively. Does the one called to leadership believe the Spirit has already been poured out or does he think he has to bestow the gift?[19]

Clerical persona

Consideration should also be given to the clerical persona of deacons. Although perhaps a minor factor in the overall context of the project, it seems germane to examine the appropriateness of the title "reverend" and the wearing of clerical attire. It may, for example, be appropriate to define "clerical dress" for deacons as the display of a suitable emblem on the lapel rather than Roman collars and dark shirts, which perhaps serve to reinforce a sacerdotal model of Holy Orders. Similarly, the use of the term "reverend" may merely restrict the understanding of what it means to be in Roman Catholic Holy Orders. If the deacon is truly a sacramental sign of seamlessness in the world of work and society at large, there seems little justification for modes of dress and address which betoken presbyteral priesthood. It would also be helpful to have consistency across the province, if not the entire Church in England and Wales, as this would minimise the risk of misunderstanding the status of the minister in attendance.

Selection and formation of deacons

It is recommended that those involved in the discernment and initial screening of candidates for the diaconate are, themselves, theologically formed in order to discern the distinctive charisms of the diaconal calling. For each aspirant to the ministry, there is clearly an invitation from God which requires a personal response. However, the ecclesial dimension of service to the people of God within Holy Orders should be a key consideration for those charged with the task of discerning the suitability of aspirants. The prospective deacon should be identifiable in his community as one who models in his home and professional life the gospel values which he is now invited to exercise on behalf of the people of God and at the behest of his bishop. It is the essential that formators and spiritual directors of deacons in training recognise that the diaconate is neither a reward for good lay ministry nor a means of bolstering sacramental provision due to a shortage of presbyters.

Final reflections

In bringing this endeavour to a close, it is fitting to reflect that, as "research in action", it began with an interest in an ecclesiological phenomenon but with no specific hypothesis to test. It was an invitation to "put out into the deep and let down the net." The catch was diverse and plentiful and some aspects could only be addressed in a perfunctory manner, since they were ancillary to the main topic. However, the presenting issues have indicated that the diaconate is a rich and complex ministry which reflects the diverse gifts of those called to this vocation. Although it serves the people of God in a way which could not have been envisaged by the Council Fathers at Vatican II, its full potential can only be realised when it ceases to be an "optional extra" at the discretion of the local ordinary and becomes a sacramental symbol of what the entire community is called to be. As Ditewig expresses it:

> The deacon stands empowered as a sign of Christ's own *kenosis*, a sign that human life is not about seeking material wealth, possessions and positions of power and domination. Rather the communion of disciples is called to empty themselves in addressing the needs of others."[20]

In this way, the ordained ministry of the deacon is the "dim reflection in the mirror" (1 Cor. 13.12) through which all can see their own call to *diakonia*.

The contemporary permanent diaconate exemplifies what the Second Vatican Council celebrated – *aggiornamento* and *ressourcement*. It is not only a restored ancient office, but a ministry reconstituted for its own time and characterised by an energetic engagement in the world in a way which is impossible for either priest or bishop. It is a ministry which can be moulded around the giftedness of the individual deacon so that all aspects of his life – home, parish and profession can witness to the call of Christ. One of the Southwark Province deacons described this witness as "primarily by being married, by living in the real world where the mortgage has to be paid, the gutters cleared, the kids' vomit mopped up, the groceries bought. By standing in the dole queue. By having sex. By suffering. Very few priests and bishops have done all that. So the people can talk to you about it, in the belief that you will understand."

In mapping a trajectory for the future of the permanent diaconate, there will be some choices to be made – whether to encourage further increases in the numbers of permanent deacons so that they are even more visible as agents of the bishop's governance, or to re-direct resources into lay formation. It is also worth noting that, as legally constituted charitable bodies, dioceses are increasingly required to give an account of themselves through trustees and other mechanisms of accountability. Strategic pastoral plans and funding frameworks therefore inform decision-making on what can and cannot be achieved. Within these structures, the priest as "lone ranger" is becoming increasingly rare and collaborative ministerial models becoming the norm. It is still a stretch for credibility to perhaps envisage strategic recruitment for specific diaconal ministries, but this may offer one means of linking the permanent deacon's role to the bishop's ministry.

Although ambiguity and confusion may still prevail about the role of the contemporary deacon, it is reassuring that the fears of those Council Fathers who envisaged that young men would simply choose the "easy way"[21] have not been realised. Instead the permanent diaconate has been embraced by mature men who have accepted what appears to be a more complex challenge of evaluating contemporary society with its drive and angst about status and success and chosen as their vocation to hold the tension between working successfully in the world whilst labouring, largely unseen, with those who are "sitting in the ashes". They have chosen to inhabit an ecclesial space in which tensions about competing roles and status are ever present. Rather than seeking to resolve these tensions, it might ultimately be more fruitful for the deacon to honour and express those tensions as part of his calling. Perhaps the metaphor of "ecclesiastical amphibian" suits him best – one who can so contextualise his ministry that he can say in the words of St Paul "For the weak, I made myself weak. I made myself all things to all men in order to save some at any cost; and I still do this, for the sake of the gospel, to have a share in its blessing" (1 Cor. 9:22-23).

The key to the future reception of the permanent diaconate and the healthy development of collaborative lay ministry lie in theologically robust formation, religious education and catechesis, without which the deacon will continue to be seen as a mini-priest, a filler of gaps or some sort of "semi-lay" man. The diaconate and indeed all Holy Orders must be seen in interrelationship. Preston describes the hierarchy as "the whole ordered body and not some group of people within the body."[22] Guiver uses the analogy of a dance partner.[23] He notes that a dance partner cannot be conceptualised without the other partner. In the context of the threefold ministry of priesthood, Guiver's analogy becomes a formation dancing team which includes lay faithful, those of other faiths and those with none – in fact all who are within the bishop's jurisdiction as the ordinary of the local Church. Within this

| Summary and the Way Ahead

dynamic, the permanent diaconate, as a sign of the seamlessness of service in the world and Church, an agent for social justice, a herald of the word, and empowering servant leader can be celebrated as a valid and vital ministry and an outpouring of self-giving love.

For personal reflection or for discussion in small groups
1. How do you envisage the future development of the permanent diaconate?
2. If a member of your family expressed an interest in becoming a permanent deacon, how would you react?

Endnotes
___

[1] Hayes, M.A. 2010. "Reclaiming the Secular and the Religious" in *Pastoral Review* Vol 6, Issue 2. March/April 2010 pp.2-3.

[2] National Vocation Office statistics indicate a 7% drop in active diocesan clergy over the period 1994-2003, a 28% decrease in ordained members of religious orders and a 29% increase in the number of retired clergy.

[3] See "Differences in Kind and Degree" issued by senior Vatican officials on 15 August 1997 http://www.vatican.va/roman_curia/pontifical_councils/laity/documents/rc_con_interdic_doc_15081997_en.htmlin accessed 13/02/2013 – Libreria Editrice Vaticana (© Libreria Editrice Vaticana, 2013).

[4] McKnight, W.S. 2006 "The Diaconate as *Medius Ordo*: Service in Promotion of Lay Participation" in J. Keating (ed). *The Deacon Reader*. New York:Paulist p.79.

[5] "The sacrament of Holy Orders..confers an indelible spiritual character and cannot be repeated or conferred temporarily" Catechism of the Catholic Church 1582. With regard to those who are no longer able to discharge the obligations and functions of orders, CCC1583 states that those in Holy Orders cannot become laymen again "in the strict sense because the character imprinted by ordination is forever. The vocation and mission received on the day of his ordination mark him permanently".

[6] Ordination to the diaconate is carried out one year before ordination to the priesthood for which the minimum age requirement is twenty five.

[7] Barnett, J.M. 1995. *The Diaconate – A Full and Equal Order*. Harrisburg: Trinity Press.p.148.

[8] The minor orders were porter, lector, exorcist and acolyte with the major orders being subdeacon, deacon, presbyter and bishop. Currently, only men may exercise the" installed" ministries of lector and acolyte.

[9] McKnight, W.S. 2001. *The Latin Rite Deacon: Symbol of Communitas and Social Intermediary among the People of God.* Pontificam Athenaum St Anselmo De Urbe. In his thesis, McKnight sums up the deacon's mediating role as one in which the deacon functions as a personal agent and promoter of charity, a role in which he is a sacramentally configured icon of Christ in a way which is distinct from the other Holy Orders. "Deacons are to be concrete manifestations of Christ among us. They represent the diaconal dimension of the church as a whole. There is a need for this sacramental presence among us." p.95.

[10] One respondent expressed it as follows, "Although I fully appreciate that this is inconsistent with diaconal orders and the sacrament, were there a way that deacons might administer a sacrament of anointing – perhaps combined with a "confession of desire", I think this could be something that would contribute positively to the diaconal ministry of charity."

[11] Osborne, K. 2006. *The Permanent Diaconate – Its History and Place in the Sacrament of Orders.* New York: Paulist Press. p.177.

[12] Ibid p.189.

[13] "Propadeutic" is the term given to the preparatory period of one year of discernment and reflection before approval as a candidate for formation.

[14] The Users Guide to the United States Conference of Catholic Bishops (USCCB) publication *Wives of Deacons, Ordinary Women, Extraordinary Lives*, describes the video and discussion resource offered as "a parish or diocesan information session on the ministry of the diaconate. It might also be used as part of the diaconate candidate formation process, or for ongoing formation after ordination". http://www.usccb.org/deacon/WivesofDeacons_ UsersGuide.pdf accessed 03/02/2010

[15] Cummings, O. F. 2004. *Deacons and the Church.* New York: Paulist Press. p.101.

[16] See also Tertullian's *De Exhortatione Castitates 7, De Monogamia 16* and *Ad Uxorem i,7.*and Origen's homily *In Lucam xvii* as noted in Chapter 8.

[17] Benedict XVI, 2009. *Omnium in Mentem* http://www.clsa.org/news/40056/Omnium-in-Mentem-English-Translation.htm accessed 28/11/2012

[18] Wilson, G.B. 2008. *Clericalism - The Death of Priesthood.* Collegeville, Minnesota: Liturgical Press. p. 125.

[19] Ibid p.131.

[20] Ditewig, W. 2006. "The Kenotic Leadership of Deacons" in Keating J. (ed) *The Deacon Reader*: New York: Crossroad. p. 274.
[21] Cardinal Spellman's comments were alluded to in Chapter 3.
[22] Preston, G. 1997. *Faces of the Church – Meditations on a Mystery and its Images*. Edinburgh: T&T Clark. p. 152
[23] Guiver, G. 2001. *Priests in a People's Church*. London: SPCK. p.vii.

Appendix A | Research Methodology

Two research methodologies were adopted for the Southwark Province project on the permanent diaconate – quantitative and qualitative.

Quantitative

Since the study did not set out to test hypotheses or measure responses within scales of satisfaction, it was felt that a limited quantitative data return was acceptable, in this case 30.8%. Also, given that the Ushaw study of 2007 had been conducted using scales of satisfaction, this provided rich results which could be called upon without replicating the exercise. The Ushaw response rate of 56 from Southwark Provincewas similar to the present project where 53 responses were achieved.

All 172 deacons in the Province were invited to participate in the research by completing a questionnaire. The questionnaire comprised six sections:

- Personal Information
- Describing your period of formation
- Describing your life as an ordained deacon
- Personal Development
- Life at home/Work
- Any other reflections

The draft questions were submitted for comment to selected "critical friends" involved in the formation and selection of candidates for the diaconate and the priesthood, including the Dean of Studies and Chair of the National Assembly of Directors and Assistant Directors of the Permanent Diaconate. The questionnaires were then submitted for approval to the College Research Ethics Committee of St Mary's University College, part of the University of Surrey.

An on-line questionnaire was considered, but rejected on the grounds of data security. It was felt that participants might not share their personal stories with confidence if they thought their narratives could be 'lost in transmission' and their identity compromised. In addition, all participants might not have had ready access to a computer or be sufficiently skilled to complete on-line returns. Instead, respondents were given the option of completing an electronic *Word* version of the questionnaire which could be attached to an email as an alternative to a paper return by post.

Demographic data extracted from the questionnaires were presented in tabular and graphical formats whilst numbers of respondents or percentages are cited in the narrative summaries e.g. "x participants did not reply to this question or "y% felt the call to ministry when they were young men." In order to encourage the respondents to name their own experience, pre-determined classifications and tick boxes were been avoided. This has inevitably resulted in a range of responses to commonly applied demographic questions like ethnic grouping. The responses to this question include "White British", "White British (Cornish)", "Caucasian", "White European" etc. Similarly, in naming their former faith allegiance, if not Roman Catholicism, there have been some unpredictable results – "Catholic/Christian Fellowship" or simply, "Baptised". These, however, do not detract from the project but rather enhance it by demonstrating that the voice of the respondent is truly heard.

As noted earlier, quantitative comparisons have been made with the findings of other diaconal research projects, in particular the Ushaw study of 2007, since this work also included the deacons of Southwark province. It was particularly pleasing to have been able to discuss the Ushaw study with its author in the formative stages of this project and his kind permission to give access to the anonymised and coded data for Southwark Province is deeply appreciated. This has enabled reflection across the disciplines of theology and social science.

Qualitative – adapted grounded theory

The primary qualitative approach for this inquiry is based on *Grounded Theory*, a method commonly employed in the social sciences. This methodology does not test pre-determined hypotheses, but instead, invites narrative responses in interviews or written accounts. These may take the form of reflective journals or, in the case of this project, questionnaires. The questionnaire was devised using mainly "open questions" to glean demographic information and invite accounts of the deacons' initial call to ministry, formation and development, the experience of the early days of ministry and the impact of ministry upon work and family life.

Using these narratives, *Grounded Theory* offers a means to identify an initial set of themes and topics which can be further developed as the research proceeds. The researcher devises sets of codes under which data can be classified and adds his/her own observations which are integrated as a set of "memos". More focused coding can then be applied as the main categories emerge from the data.

In the context of this project, a *Grounded Theory* approach was applied, but initial themes and codes were identified from the literature search. These were further developed as the data gathering proceeded and additional ad hoc codes added "in vivo". This ensured that the researcher remained open to exploring whatever theoretical possibilities were discerned in the data.[1]

The data management and analytical tool used for the project was MAXQDA 2007. This "computer assisted qualitative data analysis software" (CAQDAS) enables questionnaire data and interview transcripts to be analysed and coded and then extracted selectively for further summary.

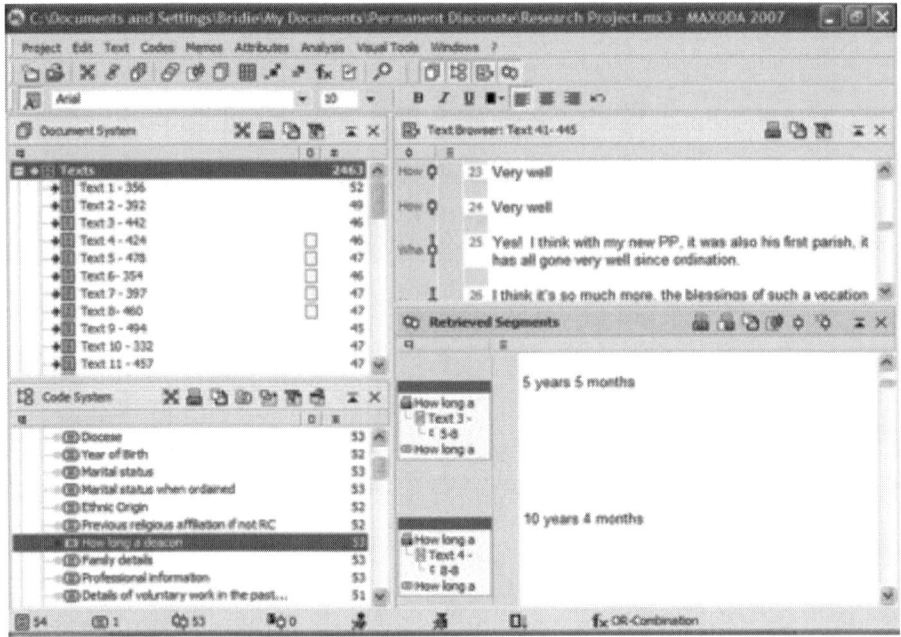

MAXQDA data access window

As can be seen from the figure above, data is accessible through a four-paned window and segments activated for extraction and summary. In the above table, the Texts shown in the top left segment comprise the transcribed accounts from the deacons. The Code System Box in the bottom left pane lists the various topics and themes. The topic highlighted ("How long a deacon") has been activated to interrogate the data and the results are listed in the box at the bottom right corner. The top right box is used to input individual texts or gain access to make amendments. Data can then be exported to a range of formats for analysis and presentation e.g. Excel spreadsheets or HTML. The analytical potential is therefore considerable and the challenge for the researcher is to ensure that, when key themes have been identified, the residual material does not divert unduly. However, it is important that the integrity of the work is not compromised through disregarding themes which, although not apparently central to the main research endeavour, may point to areas for further consideration and reflection. In this instance, the role of the deacon's wife, her formation and support are areas which call for further consideration but they were peripheral to this present research.

In testing a robust methodology for this inquiry, the following questions were felt to demand a positive response.

- Has the research achieved intimate familiarity with the setting or topic?
- Are the data sufficient to merit the claims made by the researcher?
- Are there strong links between gathered data and argument and analysis?[2]

Interviews

The interview phase of the project comprised the views of "critical friends" who, although not directly involved in Southwark Province, provided useful insights as academic theologians and formators of candidates for priesthood. The interview transcripts were subjected to an Adapted Grounded Theory analysis using MAXQDA.

Literature search

This included consideration of the earliest references to deacons in the New Testament, how their ministry evolved in the early centuries of the Church, as described by the Church Fathers, became an influential permanent ministry which then subsequently declined and became a transitional Holy Order en route to priesthood. This exploration of the ministry's heritage is crucial to the contemporary understanding of what the permanent diaconate signifies for the Church community. The recollected memory of the ministry's early foundation may, paradoxically, contribute to a misunderstanding of what it can best "deliver" in modern times, giving rise to the fundamental question: "What is the contemporary deacon called to be and called to do in the modern Church?"

Contemporary theologians, some of whom are also permanent deacons have contributed major thematic strands to the work. Collins, in seeking a definition of *diakonia* in a relevant modern context, has informed questions relating particularly to the charitable works section of the deacons' questionnaire and also raised awareness of the inherent danger in perceiving deacons as ordained social workers. The need to explore a "servant-ecclesiology" and to situate the permanent diaconate theologically in Trinitarian communion has been identified in the work of Ditewig whilst Gaillardetz invites a more fundamental consideration of the continued usefulness in the distinction between lay and clerical.

Researcher's perspective

The researcher's perspective must also be acknowledged in any research endeavour. It is impossible to conduct research, particularly of a qualitative reflective type without noting the researcher's perspective. In this sense, the research project is a "political act". Researchers and participants "make assumptions about what is real, possess stocks of knowledge, occupy social statuses and pursue purposes that influence the respective views and actions in the presence of each other".[3] There is of course no alternative, no Year Zero. In this research enterprise, the perspective is that of a Roman Catholic lay woman, who is therefore ineligible for consideration for diaconal or any other branch of Holy Orders. The wisdom or otherwise of such exclusion cannot be ignored in its entirety, but it does not relate immediately to this work. Instead, aspects of women's ministry, their continued exclusion of from Holy Orders and speculation as to future developments are reserved for the chapter entitled "Women's Diaconal Ministry".

There are, however, some advantages in undertaking theological research as a Roman Catholic lay woman. A lay researcher is not incardinated canonically to any particular diocese, although the support of the bishops was both personally affirming and helpful in gaining access to their clergy. Because of this, it was possible to adopt the role of independent "honest broker" and be entrusted with information and reflections which might not otherwise have been shared with diocesan officers or fellow -clergy. All such reflection and information were received with gratitude and respect and hopefully treated with honesty and academic integrity.

Endnotes

[1] Charmaz, K. 2006. *Constructing Grounded Theory*. London: Sage. pp.45-48.
[2] Ibid pp.182-183
[3] Ibid p.15.

BIBLIOGRAPHY

The New Jerusalem Bible 1990. London: Darton, Longman and Todd.
The Holy Bible, Authorised King James Version. London: Collins Cleartype Press.
The New Testament. 2004 translated by Nicholas King. Stowmarket: Kevin Mayhew.
Life Application Study Bible. 1996. Wheaton, Illinois: Tyndale House Publishers.
Sacrosanctum Concilium (Constitution on the Sacred Liturgy) 1963
Lumen Gentium (Dogmatic Constitution on the Church) 1964
Unitatis Redintegratio (Decree on Ecumenism) 1964
Ad Gentes (Decree on the Church's Missionary Activity) 1965
Gaudium et Spes (Pastoral Constitution on the Church in the Modern World) 1965 in Flannery, A. (ed) 1996 *Vatican Council II – Constitutions, Decrees, Declarations.* New York: Costello.
Roman Missal. 1963. Derry: McColgan.
Roman Missal Jerusalem Bible Version .1973. Newry: CBC. Distributors.
Barnett, J.M. 1995. *The Diaconate – A Full and Equal Order.* Harrisburg: Trinity Press.
Beal, J.P, J.A. Coridan and T.J. Green. 2002. New Commentary on the Code of Canon Law. New York: Paulist Press.
Bettenson, H. (ed) 1963. *The Early Christian Fathers – A Selection from the Writings of the Fathers from St Clement of Rome to St Athanasius.* Translated by H Bennenson. London: Oxford University Press.
Brown, R. 1999. *Priest and Bishop – Biblical Reflections.* Eugene, Oregon: Wipf and Stock.
Brown, R. 2005. *Being a Deacon Today.* London: Morehouse.
Browne, P. 2005. "Diaconate in the Modern Church" in *Pastoral Review*, Vol 1, Issue 5 (Sept/Oct), pp.26-28.
Catholic Bishops Conference of England and Wales. 2005. *General Instruction of the Roman Missal.* London: Catholic Truth Society.
Catholic Bishop's Conference of England and Wales. 2005. *With Hearts and Minds.* London: Catholic Truth Society.

Charmaz, K. 2006. *Constructing Grounded Theory.* London: Sage.

Coghlan, D., T. Brannick. 2005. *Doing Action Research in Your Own Organisation.* London: Sage.

Collins, J. 2002. *Deacons and the Church.* Harrisburg: Gracewing.

Congregation for the Clergy and Congregation for Catholic Education. 1998. *The Permanent Diaconate – Basic Norms for the Formation of Permanent Deacons and Directory for the Ministry and Life of Permanent Deacons.* London: Catholic Truth Society.

Congar, Y. 1960. *Laity, Church and the World* . London: Geoffrey Chapman.

Cummings, O.F. 2004. *Deacons and the Church.* New York: Paulist Press.

Cummings, O. F., W. Ditewig and R .Gaillardetz. 2005. *The Theology of the Diaconate.* New York: Paulist Press.

DePree, M. 2002. "Servant Leadership: Three Things Necessary" in Spears, L.C. and M. Lawrence (eds) 2002 Focus *on Leadership: Servant Leadership for the Twenty-First Century.* New York: John Wiley and Sons.

Dillon, R.J. in J. Fitzmyer (ed) 1991.*The New Jerome Biblical Commentary.* London: Geoffrey Chapman. pp.722-767.

Diocese of Portsmouth. 2006. *Introduction to Formation for the Permanent Diaconate in the Diocese of Portsmouth.*

Diocese of Southwark 1994. *The Permanent Diaconate in the Diocese of Southwark.*

Ditewig, W.T. 2007. *The Emerging Diaconate.* New York: Paulist Press. Ditewig, W. 2006. "The Kenotic Leadership of Deacons" in Keating J. (ed) *The Deacon Reader*: New York: Crossroad. pp.248-277.

Dolan J.P., R. S. Appleby et al 1989. *Transforming Parish Ministry.* New York: Crossroad.

Doyle, D.M. 2002. *The Church Emerging from Vatican II.* Mystic, CT: Twenty-third Publications.

Dulles, A. 1967. *Dimensions of the Church.* Westminster, Maryland: Newman Press.

Dulles, A. 1976. *Models of the Church.* Dublin: Gill and Macmillan.

Echlin, E.P. 1971. *The Deacon in the Church – Past and Future.* New York: Alba House.

Elliott, J. "The Jewish Messianic Movement – from faction to sect" in P.F. Esler (ed) 1995. *Modelling Early Christianity.* London and New York: Routledge. pp.75-96.

Fiore, B. 2003. in Harrington D. (ed) *Sacra Pagina Vol 4 The Pastoral Epistles*. Collegeville: Liturgical Press. pp 73- 83.

Foley, J. 2000. *A Road to the Permanent Diaconate including its History in Southwark 1980 – 2000*. Publisher unknown.

Frend, W.H.C. 1991. *The Early Church*. Norwich:SCM.

Fry, T. (ed) 1982. *The Rule of St Benedict in English*. Collegeville, Minnesota: The Liturgical Press.

Geary, B. and Kendall, J. 2007. "The Diaconate in Scotland, England and Wales: A demographic profile and an investigation of well-being and diaconal identity". Paper presented at Ushaw Bicentennial Colloquium: *Formation for the Future – Discovering Mutually Receptive Gifts*. Durham: England. January 2008.

Gooley, A. 2006. "*Deacons and the Servant Myth*", in *Pastoral Review*, Vol 2, Issue 6. (Nov/Dec 2006) pp.3-7.

Guiver, G. 2001. *Priests in a People's Church*. London: SPCK.

Hawkins, F. 1992. "The Didache" in Jones, C, G Wainwright et al (eds) 1992. *The Study of Liturgy*. London: SPCK. pp.84-86.

Hawkins, F. 1992. "The Tradition of Ordination in the Second Century" in Jones, C, G Wainwright et al (eds) 1992. *The Study of Liturgy*. London: SPCK. pp.347-355.

Hayes, M.A. 2010. "Reclaiming the Secular and the Religious" in *Pastoral Review* Vol 6. Issue 2. (March/April 2010) pp.2-3.

Heine, S. 1987. *Women and Early Christianity*. English translation by J. Bowden. London: SCM.

Hill, E. 1988. *Ministry and Authority in the Church*. London: Geoffrey Chapman.

Isherwood, L. and D. McEwan. 2001. *Introducing Feminist Theology*. Sheffield: Sheffield Academic Press.

Jamison, C., D. Lundy, and L. Poole. 1995. *To Live is to Change – A Way of Reading Vatican II*. Chelmsford: Rejoice Publications.

Jefford, C. 2006. *The Apostolic Fathers and The New Testament*. Peabody, Massachusetts: Hendrickson Publishers. pp.15-18.

Johnson, L.T. 2006. *The Acts of the Apostles – Sacra Pagina Series Vol 5*. Collegeville Minnesota: Liturgical Press.

Kasper, W. 1989. *Theology and Church*. London: SCM Press.

Kasper, W. 2003. *Leadership in the Church*. New York: Crossroad.

Keating, J. (ed) 2006. *The Deacon Reader*. New York: Paulist Press.

Keating, J. 2009. "Presiding at the Liturgy of Charity" in *New Diaconal Review* Issue 2 (May) pp.4-13.

Latcovich, M. 1996. *The Effects of the Ministerial Environment on RC Permanent Deacons and their Spouses*. Case Western Reserve University.

Latcovich, M. "The Diaconate and Marriage: A Sociological Reflection" in J. Keating (ed) 2006. *The Deacon Reader*. New York: Paulist Press. pp.213-231.

Macy, G. 2008. *The Hidden History of Women's Ordination*. New York: Oxford University Press.

Malina,B. J. "Early Christian Groups- Using small group formation theory to explain Christian organisations" in P.F. Esler (ed) 1995. *Modelling Early Christianity*. London and New York: Routledge. pp.96-114.

McCaslin, P and M. Lawler. 1986. *Sacrament of Service*. New York: Paulist Press.

McConvery, B.2010. The Deacon and the Ministry of the Word" in Dullea, E (ed). *2010 Deacons – Ministers of Christ and of God's Mysteries*. Dublin: Veritas. pp.49-55.

McKenzie, J.L. 1985. *Authority in the Church*. London: Geoffrey Chapman.

McKnight, W.S. 2001. *The Latin Rite Deacon: Symbol of Communitas and Social Intermediary among the People of God*. Pontificam Athenaum.S Anselmo De Urbe.

McKnight, W.S. "The Diaconate as Medius Ordo: Service in Promotion of Lay Participation" in J. Keating (ed) 2006. *The Deacon Reader*. New York: Paulist Press. pp.78-98.

McPartlan, P.2006 "The Deacon and *Gaudium et Spes*" in J. Keating (ed) 2006. *The Deacon Reader*. New York: Paulist Press. pp. 56-77.

Meehan, R. 1997. *The Emerging Role of the Deacon's Wife in the Catholic Church*. Case Western Reserve University.

Meehan, R. 2006. "The Deacon's Wife: An Emerging Role" in J. Keating (ed) 2006. *The Deacon Reader*. New York: Paulist Press. pp.232-247.

Mitchell, N. 1983. *Mission and Ministry- History and Theology in the Sacrament of Order*. Wilmington: Michael Glazier.

Müller, G. 2002. *Priesthood and Diaconate*. English translation by M.J. Miller. San Francisco: Ignatius Press.

Nowell, R. 1968. *The Ministry of Service*. London: Burns and Oates.

O'Connell Killen, P. and J. De Beer. 2004. *The Art of Theological Reflection*. New York: Crossroad.

O'Meara, F. 1983. *Theology of Ministry*. New York: Paulist Press.

Osborne, K. 1993. *Ministry – Lay Ministry in the Roman Catholic Church, Its History and Theology*. New York: Paulist Press.

Osborne, K. 2003. "Envisioning a Theology of Ordained and Lay Ministry" in S. Wood, (ed.) 2003 *Ordering the Baptismal Priesthood*. Collegeville, Minnesota: Liturgical Press, pp.196-199.

Osborne, K. 2006. *The Permanent Diaconate – Its History and Place in the Sacrament of Orders*. New York: Paulist Press.

Philips, G. 1966 in Vorgrimler H (ed) *Commentary on the documents of Vatican II*. English translation by K Smyth, L Adolphus and R Strachan. London: Burns and Oates; Herder and Herder pp 105-137.

Power, D. 2003. "Priesthood Revisited- Mission and Ministries in the Royal Priesthood" in S. Wood (ed) *Ordering the Baptismal Priesthood* 2003. Minnesota: Collegeville pp.88-103.

Preston, G. 1997. *Faces of the Church – Meditations on a Mystery and Its Images*. Edinburgh: T&T Clark.

Quasten, J., J. Plumpe (eds) 1946. *The Epistles of St Clement of Rome and St Ignatius of Antioch*. English translation by J Kleist. New York: Newman Press.

Ratigan, V.K., A.A. Swidler (eds) 1990. *A New Phoebe – Perspectives on Roman Catholic Women and the Permanent Diaconate*. Kansas City: Sheed and Ward.

Road, C. 2005. "The Permanent Diaconate in England and Wales", in *Pastoral Review* Vol.1, Issue 2, (March/April), pp.32-36.

Rolheiser, R. 2006. *Secularity and the Gospel*. New York: Crossroad Publishing Company.

Rynne, X. 1999. *Vatican Council II*. New York: Orbis Books.

Schillebeeckx, E. 1973. *The Mission of the Church*. London: Sheed and Ward.

Schillebeeckx, E. 1980. *Ministry – A Case for Change*. London: SCM.

Stagaman, D 1999. *Authority in the Church*. Collegeville, Minnesota: Michael Glazier.

Sullivan, F.A. 1996. *Creative Fidelity*. Dublin: Gill and Macmillan.

Taylor, P.J. 2007. *Called to Serve*. Twickenham: Athena.

Theissen, G. 1977. *The First Followers of Jesus*. London: SCM.

United States Conference of Catholic Bishops. 1993. "The Theology of the Restoration of the Diaconate" in *Foundations for the Renewal of the Diaconate*. Washington DC: United States Conference of Catholic Bishops 1993: 163.

Vorgrimler, H. 1966. *Commentary on the documents of Vatican II.* English translation by K Smyth, L Adolphus and R Strachan. London: Burns and Oates; Herder and Herder.
Whitehead, J.D., E.E. Whitehead. 1995. *Method in Ministry.* Oxford: Sheed and Ward.
Wijngaards, J. 2001. *The Ordination of Women in the Catholic Church – Unmasking a Cuckoo's Egg Tradition.* London: Darton, Longman and Todd.
Wijngaards Serrarens, N. 2006. *Partners in Solidarity.* Steenwiijk, Netherlands: Grafisch productiebedrijf Gorter.
Wilson, G.B. 2008. *Clericalism- The Death of Priesthood.* Collegeville, Minnesota: Liturgical Press.
Witherington, B. 1998. *The Acts of the Apostles – A Socio-Rhetorical Commentary.* Carlisle: The Paternoster Press.
Wolski Conn, J. (ed) 1986. *Women's Spirituality: Resources for Christian Development.* New York: Paulist.
Zagano, P. 2004. *Called to Serve – A Spirituality for Deacons.* Ligouri: Ligouri Publications.
Zagano, P. 2010." Inching Towards a Yes". in *The Tablet* 9 January 2010.

Electronic resources

Apostolic Constitutions Book III Section 2
> http://www.newadvent.org/cathen/15687b.htm accessed 20/11/2009.

Aquinas, T. *Summa Theologiae*
> http://www.newadvent.org/summa/3177.htm accessed 19/11/ 2009.

Ball, M. 2000. Sermon preached in Peterhouse Chapel on the Twenty-second Sunday after Trinity, 19th November 2000. http://www.pet.cam.ac.uk/chapel/ministry accessed 13/12/2010.

Beck, A. 2006. *The Compendium of the Social Doctrine of the Church.* http://www.rcsouthwark.co.uk/deacon_home.htm accessed 26/11/2007.

Benedict XVI. 2007. *Summorum Pontificum*
> http://www.ewtn.com/library/papaldoc/b16SummorumPontificum.htm accessed 09/03/2010.

Benedict XVI. 2009. *Omnium in Mentem*
> *http://www.vatican.va/holy_father/benedict_xvi/apost_letters/documents/hf_ben-xvi_apl_20091026_codex-iuris-canonici_en.html* accessed 13/04/2010.

Boeree, G. 1997 *Personality Theories- Erik Erikson.*
http://webspace.ship.edu/cgboer/erikson.html accessed 26/11/2007.

Catholic Bishops Conference of England and Wales 1998. *One Bread One Body* *http://www.catholic-ew.org.uk/catholic_church/publications* accessed 13/04/2010.

Catholic Bishops Conference of England and Wales 2007. *Catholic Directory for England and Wales Statistics 1981-2003.* http://www.catholic-ew.org.uk/cathstats/clergy.htm accessed 26/11/2007.

Cholij, R. *Priestly Celibacy in Patristics and in the History of the Church* http://www.vatican.va/roman_curia/congregations/cclergy/documents/rc_con_cclergy_doc_01011993_chisto_en.html accessed 21/07/2010 – Libreria Editrice Vaticana (© Libreria Editrice Vaticana, 2013).

Code of Canon Law. 1983.
http://www.vatican.va/archive/ENG1104/__PY.HTM accessed 20/10/09 – Libreria Editrice Vaticana (© Libreria Editrice Vaticana, 2013).

Council of Elvira. http://www.csun.edu/~hcfll004/elvira.html accessed 22/07/2010.

Council of Nicea Canon19. http://www.newadvent.org/fathers/3801.htm accessed20/11/09.

Council of Trent Canon 4.
http://history.hanover.edu/texts/trent/ct23.html accessed 13/02/13

Didache – The Teaching of the Twelve Apostles.
http://www.newadvent.org/fathers/0714.htm accessed 23/08/2010.

Dogmatic Constitution on the Church of Christ 1870
http://www.ewtn.com/library/COUNCILS/V1.htm#6 accessed 7/5/2010.

Flavius Josephus. *Jewish Antiquities*
http://www.biblestudytools.com/history/flavius-josephus/antiquities-jews/book-4/chapter-8.html?p=4 accessed 10/01/2012

Francis I. 2013. Homily at Chrism Mass, Maundy Thursday, 28 March 2013. http://www.vatican.va/holy_father/francesco/homilies/2013/documents/pa pa-francesco_20130328_messa-crismale_en.html accessed 04/06/2013 – Libreria Editrice Vaticana (© Libreria Editrice Vaticana, 2013).

Hanvey, J. and T Carroll. 2005 *On the Way to Life.*
http://www.cesew.org.uk/standard.asp?id=514 accessed 13/04/2010.

John Paul II 1988.*Mulieris Dignitatem.*
> http://www.vatican.va/holy_father/john_paul_ii/apost_letters/documents/hf_jp-ii_apl_15081988_mulieris-dignitatem_en.html accessed 13/04/2010 – Libreria Editrice Vaticana (© Libreria Editrice Vaticana, 2013).

John Paul II Address on 13 November 1998 to a symposium marking twenty years of diplomatic activity in his pontificate.
> http://www.vatican.va/holy_father/john_paul_ii/speeches/1998/november/documents/hf_jp-ii_spe_19981113_academia_en.html accessed 08/06/2009 – Libreria Editrice Vaticana (© Libreria Editrice Vaticana, 2013).

John Paul II. 1992. *Pastores Dabo Vobis.*
> http://www.vatican.va/holy_father/john_paul_ii/apost_exhortations/documents/hf_jp-ii_exh_25031992_pastores-dabo-vobis_en.htm l accessed 11/04/2010 – Libreria Editrice Vaticana (© Libreria Editrice Vaticana, 2013).

John Paul II. 1994.*Ordinatio Sacerdotalis.*
> http://www.vatican.va/holy_father/john_paul_ii/apost_letters/documents/hf_jp-ii_apl_22051994_ordinatio-sacerdotalis_en.html accessed 13/04/2010 – Libreria Editrice Vaticana (© Libreria Editrice Vaticana, 2013).

Kelly, J. and E. Hemrick *Conclusions Drawn from the 1994-1995 Permanent Diaconate Study..* http://www.jknirp.com/diacon.htm accessed 26/11/2007.

Kirby, P. (ed). *Early Christian Writings*
> <http://www.earlychristianwritings.com
> http://www.earlychristianwritings.com/text/ignatius-magnesians-roberts.html accessed 06/02/2012

http://www.earlychristianwritings.com/text/ignatius-trallians-roberts.html accessed 06/02/2012

http://www.earlychristianwritings.com/text/ignatius-philadelphians-roberts.html accessed 06/02/2012

National Vocations Office http://www.ukvocation.org/callings/perm.html accessed 13/04/2010.

Paul VI. 1967 *Sacrum Diaconatus Ordinem.*
> http://www.vatican.va/holy_father/paul_vi/motu_proprio/documents/hf_p-vi_motu-proprio_19670618_sacrum-diaconatus_en.html accessed 08/04/2010 – Libreria Editrice Vaticana (© Libreria Editrice Vaticana, 2013).

Paul VI. 1972. *Ministeria Quaedam.* http://www.ewtn.com/library/PAPALDOC/P6MINORS.HTM accessed 13/04/2010.

Paul VI 1972. *Ad Pascendum -Containing Norms for the Order of Diaconate.* http://www.deacons.net/Documents/Ad_Pascendum.htm accessed 13/04/2010.

Paul VI 1976 *Inter Insigniores Declaration On The Question Of Admission Of Women To The Ministerial Priesthood.* http://www.papalencyclicals.net/Paul06/p6interi.htm accessed 23/11/2009.

Pontifical Council for Justice and Peace. *Compendium of Social Doctrine* http://www.vatican.va/roman_curia/pontifical_councils/justpeace/documents/rc_pc_justpeace_doc_20060526_compendio-dott-soc_en.html accessed 09/04/2010 – Libreria Editrice Vaticana (© Libreria Editrice Vaticana, 2013).

Pius IX. 1874. *On the Church in Austria.* http://www.papalencyclicals.net/Pius09/p9vixdum.htm accessed 06/02/2012.

Pius XI 1925 *Quas Primas* http://www.vatican.va/holy_father/pius_xi/encyclicals/documents/hf_p-xi_enc_11121925_quas-primas_en.html accessed 06/04/2010 – Libreria Editrice Vaticana (© Libreria Editrice Vaticana, 2013).

Pius XII. 1943. *Mystici Corporis Christi* http://www.vatican.va/holy_father/pius_xii/encyclicals/documents/hf_p-xii_enc_29061943_mystici-corporis-christi_en.html accessed 09/03/2010 – Libreria Editrice Vaticana (© Libreria Editrice Vaticana, 2013).

Pius XII 1947 *Sacramentum Ordinis* http://www.papalencyclicals.net/Pius12/P12SACRAO.HTM accessed 06/04/2010.

Pius XII 1957 *Guiding Principles of the Lay Apostolate* – Address to the Second World Congress of the Lay Apostolate in Rome on October 5, 1957 http://www.papalencyclicals.net/Pius12/P12LAYAP.HTM accessed 20/01/2010.

Synod of Bishops. XI Ordinary General Assembly. 2002. *The Eucharist: Source And Summit of The Life And Mission Of The Church* http://www.vatican.va/roman_curia/synod/documents/rc_synod_doc_20040528_lineamenta-xi-assembly_en.html accessed 13/04/2010 – Libreria Editrice Vaticana (© Libreria Editrice Vaticana, 2013)

Synod of Bishops. XII Ordinary General Assembly. 2007 *The Word of God on the Life and Mission of the Church* http://www.vatican.va/roman_curia/synod/documents/rc_synod_doc_20070427_lineamenta-xii-assembly_en.html accessed 13/04/2010 – Libreria Editrice Vaticana (© Libreria Editrice Vaticana, 2013).

United States Conference of Catholic Bishops 2004. *Wives of Deacons, Ordinary Women, Extraordinary Lives – Online Users Guide*, http://www.usccb.org/deacon/WivesofDeacons_ UsersGuide.pdf accessed 03/02/2010.

US Department of Defense News Briefing 12 February 2002 http://www.defense.gov/transcripts/transcript.aspx?transcriptid=2636 accessed 18/06/2013.

Wansbrough, H. 2005 Catholic Communications Network Press release of the lecture of Dom Henry Wansbrough. http://www.catholic-ew.org.uk/ccb/content/pdf/774 accessed 09/07/2009.

Other resources

United States Conference of Catholic Bishops 2004. Video "Wives of Deacons, Ordinary Women, Extraordinary Lives". Washington DC: USCCB Publishing.